MARRIAGE
THAT WORKS

CLIFF POWELL, GRAHAM BARKER
& IAN HARVEY

MARRIAGE
THAT WORKS

AN ALBATROSS BOOK

© Cliff Powell, Graham Barker and Ian Harvey, 1996

Published in Australia and New Zealand by
Albatross Books Pty Ltd
PO Box 320, Sutherland
NSW 2232, Australia
in the United States of America by
Albatross Books Pty Ltd
PO Box 131, Claremont
CA 91711, USA
and in the United Kingdom by
Lion Publishing plc
Peter's Way, Sandy Lane West
Oxford OX4 5HG, England

First edition 1996

National Library of Australia
Cataloguing-in-Publication data

Powell, Cliff, 1944-.
Marriage that works: building a loving, lasting relationship

ISBN 0 7324 1034 7

1. Marriage. 2. Interpersonal relations. I. Barker, Graham, 1946-.
II. Harvey, Ian James, 1930-. III. Title.

306.872

Cover photograph: Graham Horner
Printed and bound in Australia by Griffin Paperbacks, Netley, SA

Contents

Foreword

WHAT AM I DOING WRITING THE *FOREWORD* to another book on building good marriages? Simply
answered, I like the book! More to the point, though,
there is always a place for a good, practical guide to help
people improve their marriages — and this is one of the
best.

In the climate of the nineties, there is a move back to
basics, the core issues and values that make us tick. Cold,
pragmatic approaches, often built primarily on self-interest,
have not met the challenges that modern couples face.
There is a growing interest in linking together the spiritual
dimension of relationships and the practical 'how-to's'.

Marriage that Works is a significant and valuable contribution to this area of need. Cliff Powell, Graham
Barker and Ian Harvey have written a book that stands
out because it is practical, yet it is earthed in the undeniable
spiritual dimensions of human functioning. All committed Christians, they have built from biblical teaching,
integrating this with sound relational principles to produce
a book that meets the challenge. They hit the crucial areas
that bend marriages out of shape — the past, communication patterns, anger, sexuality, unforgiveness and so on —
and offer lines of growth.

It is apparent that they do not write from oases of
theory, but from the reality of their own marriages and

their years of clinical experience. As you read *Marriage that Works*, you will learn what makes relationships grow, the techniques that facilitate that growth and what to do to prevent 'the wheels falling off'.

Marriage that Works is an excellent handbook of tools for improving and keeping marriages in a healthy condition. Besides discussion statements for personal, couple and group use, there are techniques, suggestions and encouragement for those whose aim is a more satisfying relationship.

One last plus. *Marriage that Works* avoids the jargon that so often clouds the message. Whether you are anticipating marriage, wanting to improve your marriage or looking to work your way out of a crisis, *Marriage that Works* has something for you.

Paul Meier MD
Co-founder of Minirth-Meier Clinics, USA
1996

Introduction

THERE IS EVIDENCE TO SUGGEST that we are currently suffering a blowout in the ozone layer of marriage. For every ten marriages occurring in the Western world today, four end in separation or divorce. That is tragic. Even so, it is only part of the story.

We now have a picture of what takes place in the six marriages that don't end in divorce. They keep it going, but we would be wrong if we assume that they're all experiencing Nirvana! Some just 'stay together for the children'. Others keep up appearances because it's socially expedient, but there is no life, no genuine intimacy — just more keeping-up appearances.

Outwardly, it looks like a marriage. Inwardly, it feels like a plate of cold sago! Husband and wife tolerate or endure, but they don't enjoy. The sad truth is that only one or two out of every ten marriages achieve what we might call genuine intimacy — a close, loving relationship. There is a huge cost in personal misery associated with marriages that don't grow!

But the costs are not limited just to the adults. Un-avoidable evidence has now accumulated to show that children of divorce and children of parents who fight a lot pay a price, too. Nolen-Hoeksema, Girgus and Seligman followed 400 third-grade children and their families over a period of five years in the Princeton-Penn Longitudinal

Study in the United States. Children from divorced families and families where the parents fought a lot were significantly more depressed than children from stable, intact families. And these effects seem to maintain over time. They don't easily go away!

Further, such children experience less friendliness from other children at school, fail subjects more and have a three-and-a-half times greater chance of being hospitalised in the ensuing few years than other children! And the list of hidden costs goes on.

And how can we begin to estimate the social cost of divorce and unfulfilling marriages? Just try adding to the equation factors such as lost work-time associated with relationship crises, accidents because of worry over the state of marriages, suicides and medical problems arising from the stresses and pressures.

Perhaps you'll excuse us for feeling that there aren't a lot of things more important than putting together some practical guidelines on how to build fulfilling marriages! We don't want to overdo the bad news. However, it's very important not to fool ourselves and ignore it. We need to face reality if we want to see change.

The amazing thing is that, in spite of all the bad press, marriage is still an incredibly popular dream for most people. Anyone who, for any reason at all, fronts a classroom of young people today and asks them if they hope to get married will rapidly discover that overwhelmingly they do. Dreams, in some respects, *are* stronger than reality.

But before we leave the issue, it is worth asking why marriage is in such desperate shape. Certainly, any serious attempt to answer that question would have to look at a whole host of factors, particularly the increased financial pressures faced by families and the ever-accelerating expectations of our consumer-dominated societies.

Some twenty years ago, most married couples could anticipate owning their own home on the basis of a single income. Those days appear to have passed. Most couples now face monumental difficulties paying off a mortgage with both of them working. Clearly, these pressures have built significantly.

But the determined assault of the media on traditional marriage should not go unrecognised when we look for somewhere to pin the rap. Michael Medved, co-host of the American program *Sneak Previews*, in a disturbing analysis of today's films, notes:

> *According to the Census Bureau, two-thirds of all American adults are currently married, but movies today focus over-whelmingly on single people. If you want to test this premise, all you have to do is pick up a copy of any metropolitan newspaper and read the entertainment section to see what's currently playing at your local theatres. The number of films about single people will outnumber the films about married people by a ratio of five or six to one. And even those relatively rare films that do make an attempt to show life within a family will most often depict a marriage that is radically dysfunctional. . .*
>
> *Apparently, some stern decree has gone out from the upper reaches of the Hollywood establishment that love between married people must never be portrayed on screen. If a wedding occurs in the course of a film, it invariably marks the conclusion of a romance, never the beginning or the middle of the love relationship. . .*
>
> *With its single-minded focus on unmarried characters, the movie industry conveys the idea that it's exciting to live on your own, but boring and stifling to live within a marriage. The unspoken assumption is that married people never experience anything that's interesting enough to be dramatised in a feature film. . .*[1]

Perhaps we should not be surprised that marriages are in trouble. Perhaps the real surprise is that, with such a concerted assault, any marriages make it!

The good news is that marriage is still the best option. No society in history has come up with a better plan than a man and woman committing themselves to live together in a covenant relationship and seeking to raise children in the security that this offers. Wherever a couple has built from this foundation and done it right, you'll find a couple who are married — and loving it!

This book is written because we are unashamedly committed to marriage and we want to play a part in teaching people how to strengthen their marriages.

Part A focuses on laying the foundations. Key foundation principles *do* exist — and they are not too difficult to understand. They probably wouldn't even be so hard to put into practice if we were not constantly being overdosed by media messages which contradict them! These foundation principles are very practical. An opportunity is provided for you to do some personal assessment to see how you're doing in laying these foundations.

In Part B, we focus on building. We seek here to develop an understanding of some key building materials for fulfilling marriage. These include realistic expectations, learning to be intimate and enjoying sexual love.

Part C centres on maintenance. Everything deteriorates without some TLC from time to time — and marriage is no exception. The Second Law of Thermodynamics, sometimes called the Entropy Law, holds true for marriage also. In overly-simplistic terms, things run down. Only with specific attention will a marriage continue to be fulfilling or, better still, grow. This section aims to equip readers with specific ways of maintaining a fulfilling marriage. Chapters focus, for example, on communications skills and conflict management and just plain having fun!

Part D looks at the need for storm-proofing. Every marriage gets hit with some crises. Not infrequently, this is when things fall apart and the couple decide to quit. We set out to provide practical guidance for getting through these with the roof still on your marriage.

Each of us writes out of personal experience of the goodness that we have found in marriage. While we still don't like to think of ourselves as old (!), the plain fact is that between the three of us we have clocked up around ninety years of monogamous and incredibly rich marriage. And we like to think we're normal, so we figure if we can do it, you can, too.

But we also write out of years of clinical experience, working to help people 'real-ise' the incredible potential that God has given them in their marriage. We have found the tools that we offer here to be tools that work. We have certainly all had our failures in counselling and see that one or both of the partners really wanted a marriage without the work of building. So they opted for an alternative: another partner or no marriage at all — something on the other side of the fence.

Each of us, too, recognises that there is a spiritual dimension to marriage. It's more than a union of schedules, possessions and bodies. We bring into marriage that central part of our being, which we can only call 'spirit'. It is that aspect of each of us which relates to God. You'll find reference to the need to develop spiritually as a couple and some guidance on this throughout our book.

Our hope is that through the instruction in this book you, too, will be helped to build a marriage that really works well and one that is fulfilling beyond your wildest dreams with the partner you have chosen.

Cliff Powell
Graham Barker
Ian Harvey

Endnote
1. *Imprimis,* February 1991, p.4

Part A:
Laying the foundations

1

Leave your past life

THEY WERE DESPERATE. VINCE AND ROSEANNE had flown from their home interstate to consult me. Vince was a successful engineer with a busy consultancy. Roseanne was a sales manager. They had been married for seventeen years, had two children and yet, now, their marriage was on its last legs.

As we met over the ensuing week, their story poured out. Both agreed that their sexual relationship was the central issue. This aspect of their relationship had always been poor. Roseanne ran away briefly on their honeymoon and reported having great difficulty letting Vince get close physically. She avoided letting him hug, touch or kiss her most of the time.

They reported that they had last made love in an enjoyable way almost two years before. They had not made love at all in the last eight months because Roseanne had decided 'it wasn't worth it'. Vince had come to the end of his patience and, although he loved his wife dearly, was ready to leave. Still, Roseanne seemed unable to make any change.

I spent time alone with each of them during the week. As Roseanne shared details of her upbringing and family life, it became apparent that, although there was no clear evidence of actual sexual interference, her father had had trouble handling his sexual feelings in relation to her. He

had dominated and ruled the household with little understanding or regard for the needs of the other members.

Roseanne looked back on many of her father's actions
with deep bitterness. She could not remember him ever
praising her as a child. In fact, when she had clearly done
the best work in the Sunday School class he taught, other
children were praised instead and the prize was awarded
to someone else. He had refused to go guarantor for her
when she had an opportunity to go to university and so
she was unable to take up the offer. When she and Vince
wanted to get married, his first question to her was a
deeply hurtful: 'Why? Are you pregnant?'

But the most significant incidents appeared to be that
as the children had grown up, their father had frequently
encouraged them to fight with each other and then, when
they had a full head of steam, would intervene again and
insist that they 'kiss and make up'. He had also demanded
that Roseanne give him a kiss whenever she left the house
or as soon as she arrived back home. This was required even
when she was a young adult. She had resented this deeply.

I am not sure what my exact words were, but they
were along these lines: 'Can you see, Roseanne, what has
happened? From your father you learned a pattern of
linking acts of physical tenderness, such as kissing, with
being controlled by someone else — someone you didn't
like. Now in your marriage, you have continued the same
emotional response. You have reacted to Vince's acts of
tenderness as though he is someone seeking to control you,
when the truth is he is your husband and the one you
have *chosen* to love. He isn't your father.'

Roseanne began to cry as I was speaking. She looked
up at me with tears running down her face. 'That's it,
isn't it?' she said. 'That's what has been happening all
these years.' Both she and I believed that God listens
when we pray, so together we prayed for a breaking of

the old emotional response pattern that was triggered by Vince's acts of tenderness.

This act of prayer was a trigger. She recognised that she had to let go of the resentment at her father and mother. Once she did this, she had a new freedom. At our next session, she reported that she had gone home to Vince that day a new woman. They made love for the first time in eight months and she had felt a new freedom in giving and responding to her husband's tenderness.

Over the next weeks, it was as though they were given the honeymoon that they had never really had before. Both of them were radiant and overjoyed at this new release.

✠ Leave the parental home when practicable

The story of Roseanne and Vince underlines the importance of leaving the parental relationship, a leaving that needs to take place at a number of levels. The most obvious way is setting up one's own home. Most often, if we have not already left our parents' home before we marry, we move out when we marry. We rent a unit or house because we recognise that we are establishing a new family. Occasionally, circumstances such as the need to save may cause us to stay in the family home for a while, but we know that this is not ideal and we aim to make our move as soon as it is practicable.

There is wisdom in the call to geographically leave our parents. It is an early step in cementing the new relationship of marriage and providing a tacit recognition to ourselves, our parents and others of the primacy of the new relationship.

But the concept of leaving has wider significance. It reminds us that there are changes required in a number of other important areas of our lives.

✠ **Leave behind invalid messages and lessons**
Not all families of origin are healthy. Some are very dysfunctional and destructive — and none is totally healthy. We can see that some aspects of Roseanne's family were quite dysfunctional, so that the lessons passed on to her about tender physical contact were very destructive. The message she learned through her father's twisted actions was that kissing and physical tenderness were connected with being controlled. She failed to learn that, between a husband and wife, these actions were intended to be a beautiful prelude to the expression of love and willing self-giving in sexual intimacy.

Roseanne had to leave the distorted lesson from her father in order to learn this completely new lesson. However, as God freed her to learn the new, so she was set free to discover a closeness with Vince that she had never before known.

It is vital for each of us to take some kind of inventory of the messages we have learned from our family of origin in order to judge their usefulness or potential destructiveness for our own marriage. The most important of these lessons, in terms of the impact they can have on our marriage, will be lessons about major aspects of our own self, others, the world, relationships, God, marriage, love, sex and so on. Lessons about the correct way to squeeze the toothpaste tube, or how to celebrate Christmas properly, may cause some initial disagreement for a newly-married couple, but they will not have the same potentially explosive or corrosive power as the issues mentioned above.

Take, for example, a young man raised in a dysfunctional home with an alcoholic parent. He may well have learned the following kinds of lessons:

* I am no good; there is something wrong

with me; I'm not lovable.
* People aren't to be trusted; they let you down; they can hurt you, so don't let yourself get too close.
* Marriage just exists so you can get as much as you can; demand your rights and get your way by violence, if necessary!
* Don't share your feelings; in fact, don't even acknowledge to yourself or others that you have feelings.

Or take the case of Guy. He was a young man struggling with huge inferiority feelings in his marriage. Raised on a farm, he had always been victimised by his parents and siblings. He recalled an incident in kindergarten when he was ridiculed in front of others by a 'big' second-grader for playing on his own. When we talked through the experience, he was able to see that through this and other experiences with his family, he had taken on board messages such as 'There's something wrong with me' and 'People can hurt you'.

These two examples contain a very destructive set of messages and 'life-lessons' with which to enter marriage. Yet this may be almost exactly the kinds of life messages passed on to you by your parents, if you were raised in a dysfunctional family. Can you see how vital it is that you understand what was passed on to you, in order to evaluate it? A knowledge of these messages will help equip you to build a good marriage.

At this point, let me encourage you to work through the questionnaire at the end of this chapter. It will direct your attention to the 'life messages' passed on to you by your parents and/or childhood. When you have completed it, look over your answers and ask yourself: 'Is this a constructive or destructive message for me to be carrying in my marriage? If I live by this, will it enable me and my spouse to grow in love, or will it destroy love?'

It is important to recognise, however, that parental messages taken into our marriage are not always or necessarily bad. Many may be helpful and valid. If our family has been a reasonably healthy family then, hopefully, we will have learned many lessons that will be valuable in our own marriage. These lessons may well include how to speak respectfully, how to handle anger, how to express caring, how to sort through disagreements and conflict, how to discipline children lovingly, how to have fun, how to undertake a task, how to relate in friendship, how to give and receive and many other such lessons. Whether directly taught, or indirectly 'caught' from our parents, if these lessons are valid, then they are treasure that we bring with us into marriage.

In fact, we can go further and say, with confidence, that: 'It is *vital* for each of us to take some kind of inventory of messages we have learned from our family of origin in order to judge their usefulness or potential destructiveness for our own marriage.' I have argued here for discerning the good from the bad messages, not excising messages altogether.

✠ Leave behind past roles

But when we move into marriage, it is equally vital that we leave *behind* certain roles. Prior to marriage, we have held the role of a single person, with its opportunities for a certain quality of freedom and self-focus. The call in marriage is clearly to focus on the role of marriage partner, spouse or, as earlier forms of language expressed it, 'helpmeet'. We give up the role of single person in order to take up the new role of married person — one who is pledged to love the partner we have taken and to consider his or her interests before all others.

Learning to leave singleness is not easy. Typically, marriages struggle a little in the early years over this issue. There are often attempts to work out a 'reasonable deal' — she will do the washing, ironing and much of the cleaning; he will do the vacuuming, the dishes, clean the bathroom; and they both will share the cooking and the yard work.

There are attempts to sort out whether or not they will have some time just for themselves. Can he still play cards with a few mates every second Tuesday? Is it okay for her to continue as captain of the netball team, thus taking Saturday afternoon out of their shared time? How can they get it 'fair'? The difficulty of working out 'coupleness' in place of singleness often leads to conflict.

It is not uncommon to find that, when the first signs of marital stress begin to emerge, this is the issue in focus. The couple are, in fact, finding it hard to leave singleness. They don't realise that building a marriage will enter into their personal desires and wants quite so much. They are feeling a little cheated. She expects this of me and he expects this of me; somehow, it seems a bit unfair and some resentment begins to build.

Such couples need reassurance. They need to know that, yes, there is a significant cost if we are to achieve the intimacy that we want. We *do* have to leave the self-focussed life of a single person — and that takes some adjustment and some learning.

But the benefits are there. We were made for loving relationship and when, through marriage, we begin to achieve that quality of special closeness with another, it is a wonderful gift, a great blessing. The special task of marriage is not to lose our singleness, or deny our individuality altogether, but to give a new primacy to discovering our coupleness, learning how to sacrificially deny our own desires for love of our spouse.

✠ Leave behind the primacy of past relationships

Along with leaving singleness, we are called to leave the primacy of past relationships, especially those of son or daughter in our family of origin. We do not cease to be a son or daughter from our family of origin when we marry, but we are called upon to leave those relationships as being the most important in our life. Now that we are married, we are primarily a husband or wife and only secondarily a son or daughter in our parents' family. Most of the time this will not present a problem. However, in some marriages it may.

Elsie and Ray had such a marriage. Ray wanted to sell up and move to the country to take up a small business, but Elsie wouldn't hear of it. There was no way that she was prepared to leave the city where her parents lived. For years, Ray 'put up with it', but resentment grew and eventually he gave her an ultimatum. She still wouldn't budge and so the marriage ended. Sadly, there were children involved and they carried considerable hurt with them, not understanding why their parents had separated.

What had gone wrong? While there was clearly wrong on both sides and Ray had certainly failed to help Elsie to feel the security that she needed in the marriage, I believe it started with Elsie's failure to understand this crucial aspect of leaving. She had entered marriage, but had not left the relationship of daughter to her parents, in order to take up her new primary relationship of wife to Ray.

Conflict situations arise in this area, especially in new marriages. One or other of the newly-married couple has never understood that this new relationship requires a leaving of the old. Perhaps a parent has controlled them by guilt in the past and now he or she continues to do this. They are made to feel guilty because they no longer give their parent as much time. They are forced into situations where they have to choose between parent or spouse.

It is incredibly important to recognise from the outset that marriage requires this leaving, this re-setting of relationship priorities. And where a parent or parents need the same re-education, this needs to be done — with love, but firmly. Guilt may be experienced, but if the difficult task has been done in love, then guilt is not appropriate. The primary relationship with our spouse needs to be acted upon.

Sometimes in counselling, I find someone who is struggling with guilt over the issue of leaving a previous relationship with a brother or sister. This may be a particular stress with twins, when one of them marries. However, it can occur with any siblings who have been particularly close.

Kelly and Katelyn were sisters, and closest friends. Katelyn was happy for Kelly when she fell in love with Timothy. However, as the romance took more and more of Kelly's time, and Katelyn hardly seemed to see Kelly now, resentment began to build. Kelly began to feel pressure from her sister and found herself feeling guilty when she and Timothy went out. What should have been a period of life chockful of joy was still joyful, but it was marred by a feeling that she was failing Katelyn, that she was letting her sister down.

When the problem emerged in a premarital counselling session with Timothy and Kelly, it was already an issue that had caused much distress for Kelly and more than one argument between her and Timothy. We were able to talk it through so that Kelly could see that what was occurring was normal — in fact, even necessary. She was able to come to a point that, rather than being wrong, the change was necessary for the establishment of a new family for herself and Timothy. Together, we worked out a plan so that she could talk the issue through with Katelyn — and this she did. It was a healing, reassuring time and led to the two sisters planning ways of giving some ongoing attention to their future relationship, while they came to accept the importance of it changing.

The first building-block in marriage, then, is leaving the past life. Once that is in position, we are able to make our commitment to love our spouse, thus beginning the journey towards intimacy.

Before going on to the next chapter where we discuss commitment, use the following questionnaire to help you identify important focuses for leaving, from your past.

Questions for thought and discussion

✠ PERSONAL INVENTORY

In chapter 1, the emphasis is on the initial task of leaving behind any invalid or dysfunctional messages, or 'life lessons' that may have been passed on to us by our family of origin, or by events and circumstances that occurred in the early years of our life.

To the extent that these are *not* left behind, to that extent we will struggle unnecessarily in developing a solid foundation for our marriage. So it is important to begin this kind of personal inventory, bringing to mind those messages which have been barriers to intimacy, together with an understanding of how they were passed on to us in our early life.

Consider the following questions, recording your answers as you go.

Self

1. What messages — through specific situations, actions or words spoken to me — was I given about:
   a. my worth as a person?
   b. my worth in comparison to others?
   c. my reason for existing?
   d. my intelligence?
   e. my looks?
   f. my rights?
   g. my feelings?

2. Specifically, where did these messages come from? (List situations, actions or words spoken to you.)

Other people

3. What messages was I given about:
   a. the worth of other people?
   b. the rights of other people?
   c. the trustworthiness of other people?
   d. the safeness of other people?

4. Specifically, where did these messages come from?

The world around

5. What messages was I given about:
   a. the safeness of the world?
   b. the value of the world?

6. Specifically, where did these messages come from?

Other important life areas

7. What messages was I given about:
   a. God?
   b. marriage?
   c. love?
   d. sex?
   e. anger?
   f. how to speak to others?
   g. how to handle arguments/conflict?
   h. how to discipline children?
   i. how to express caring?
   j. how to have fun?
   k. how to give and receive?
   l. how to relate in friendship?
   m. how to undertake a task?
   n. how to react to pain or discomfort?

8. Specifically, where did these messages come from?

Checking out my life messages

9. Put an asterisk alongside each of the messages above which you recognise as being dysfunctional, in that they block you in some way from building a healthy, intimate marriage. (Note that it is important to test each of the messages by your intellect, or reasoning, rather than your feelings. Often, life messages that have been burnt into us in our early years 'feel' true, even though they make no rational sense.)

10. Now get hold of a blank sheet of paper and try your hand at re-writing the messages that you have marked with an asterisk. For example, if the message about your worth as a person was something

like 'There's something wrong with me. I'm no good', you will need to re-phrase it to something like: 'I am a person made in the image of God, therefore I am precious and of great worth.'

11. Review your life messages, and the new truths that you are seeking to live by, with your marriage partner. He or she may add to the messages you have recognised as invalid, or may help you in the task of developing replacement messages which aid the process of deepening your marriage relationship.

These are important steps in leaving our dysfunctional messages behind. We cannot let go of anything that we do not recognise as erroneous. And we cannot let go of it unless we have an alternative, which is truth, to take hold of.

The bad news is that destructive messages which have been powerfully reinforced in us by our parents and our upbringing usually are not easy to change. The good news is that they can be changed, if we work at it with determination, supporting each other, and praying for God's strength to help us.

✠ SHARING WITH YOUR LIFE PARTNER
It will be helpful to use the stimulus questions above, and the messages that you and your partner have identified, as the basis for significant communication. Make time to share with each other about the experiences that produced these messages and to *listen* to each other. Make time to help each other in the process of changing any that need change.

✠ GROUP WORK

12. Having written out your childhood messages and developed replacement truths, take the time to share in your group one or more of the dysfunctional messages that your upbringing left you with.

13. What roles that were part of your pre-marriage life do you see as not fitting well with marriage? Share any that you have found difficult to leave behind. What has helped you?

14. What changes has marriage effected in your relationships with your parents? With your brothers and/or sisters? How hard was it for you to do the necessary leaving in these areas?

2

Develop a long-term commitment

IF LEAVING OUR PAST LIFE is the first task required in setting the foundations for a fulfilling marriage in place, the second task is what we might identify as remaining committed. Unfortunately, the idea of remaining deeply committed to your marriage partner isn't all that new or sensational, so it tends to get little coverage in the popular media. Films, magazines, newspapers and TV shows all tend to distort strongly to the opposite viewpoint — explicitly stating, or implying, that cheating is more fun than staying faithful to your marriage partner and that there are no serious repercussions to deal with.

Such a view would simply be pathetic if it didn't continue to be so damaging in people's marriages and lives.

The trouble is that we human beings, despite our enlightened times, don't handle infidelity — casual commitment — well. We always feel an implied value judgment about ourselves when our marriage partner breaks faith with us. We feel hurt, ripped off, unfairly treated — and a host of insecurities rise up within us. We find it difficult to trust again, to give ourselves without reservation in intimacy.

When the media says, 'It's no big deal', our guts don't believe them. Something in us *knows* that remaining committed and faithful to our husband or wife is a crucial foundation to a lifelong, fulfilling marriage.

The trouble is that the media message is powerful and insistent. We continue to be assaulted by glamorous affairs and casual relationship models, all presented with considerable dishonesty. Little depiction is given of the shattered lives, the loneliness, the tears, the trail of destruction left in children, parents, grandparents and friends' lives. Media presentations of non-commitment in marriage rarely detail the financial costs, the loss in personal and national productivity, as people struggle to deal with their feelings in the wake of marital betrayal.

Under this sort of relentless attack, the 'simple' task of remaining committed to another person while working to build a life together soon reveals itself to be anything but easy.

This certainly was the case with Jim and Yvonne. Theirs was the storybook romance: a meeting at a church function, instant attraction and mutual affection. Within twelve months, the courtship rituals were enacted, the engagement and marriage celebrations completed and the happy couple got down to the business of getting to know each other. Leaving home seemed a breeze to the now daunting task of becoming an actual functioning unity. The functional unity looked more like a pair of one-legged unicyclists, so the questions were asked:

* What had been overlooked?
* Where was the missing piece — or pieces?
* What happened to the shared conviction that 'our love will get us through'?

Jim and Yvonne soon realised what many young couples reluctantly come to see as reality — that working for a deeply committed unity is complex and involves far more than 'moving in' and 'sharing my life'. There are a number of important elements:

* A couple takes responsibility *for* each other's welfare, growth and dignity.
* A couple shares a trust *in* each other in terms of honesty, fidelity and vulnerability.
* A couple makes a commitment *to* each other in an exclusive relationship.

It is as a couple lays foundations in these areas that the fusion, the expressive unity without loss of personal identity, comes into being.

✠ Build commitment by becoming responsible for each other

If the couple is really to remain committed, then the mutual caring responsibilities need to be understood. There is a note of warning to be sounded here. Mutual responsibility is *not* the same as assuming responsibility for things another person should assume for themselves. Such behaviour is actually irresponsible and is destructive to a relationship. The mutual responsibility emphasised here is that which promotes the partner's welfare, growth and dignity, protects these, and consciously resists doing anything that would harm the other person's welfare, growth and dignity.

This is difficult. We are all imperfect, a little 'broken around the edges'. We live in an imperfect world with other people who all have their share of brokenness. It is our natural tendency to serve ourselves and use others whenever needed. Only when we honestly face our inbuilt tendency to selfishness and 'wanting things our way' can we ever really make strides in changing. And, like the alcoholic, we will need to acknowledge that we are relatively powerless to do this sort of internal reconstruction without the help of a Higher Power.

This requires building our spiritual life — learning to draw upon strength from God. Only then can we hope to fully realise this mutual caregiving. This is not an excuse to give up on ourselves or our mate if we or they fail, but rather a statement of hope that it is possible to ground our marriage relationships in ongoing commitment. But we will need help.

In the case of Jim and Yvonne, the desire to take caring responsibility for each other's deep needs was very shallow. They promised to do so in theory, but they were products of the new society and, in practice, they were both quite committed to looking after themselves first. It is hard for a single person to learn mutual caring and selfless sharing and Jim and Yvonne had not made much progress in these areas.

The closest Jim had come to this experience was the relationship he had with his first car, an iridescent green Commodore to which he was utterly devoted. Even Yvonne was jealous of it. When Yvonne and Jim were dating, it was more a sharing of 'commons' and very rarely an accommodation to the other person's needs. The thought of seeking after the other's welfare, growth and dignity was foreign, even though the words went with their beliefs.

Many people discuss the loss of such caring attitudes as being typical of our times. Everything is electronic, quadrophonic and egocentric. But the pattern of the times is often faulty.

No era has presented us with a perfect model of relating, but there are always some good examples around if we care to look.

One such example is in the biblical story of Ruth and Boaz.

Ruth was a Moabite widow living with her Israelite mother-in-law in Israel among rural peoples. Ruth and Boaz (a blood relative of her mother-in-law Naomi) met when Ruth was gleaning in Boaz's fields. What occurred then evidenced careful respect and mutual responsibility. Boaz ensured Ruth was given fair and generous treatment and protection simply because she had the need and was a woman of good reputation and caring spirit. Ruth in turn gave Boaz respect and honoured his integrity, while making her needs known to him.

Both identified, preserved and enhanced each other's stature as persons before any relationship was established. Such a healthy foundation enabled their marriage to be fulfilling and fruitful, and provided a basis for remaining committed to one another.

Look for your own models of couples taking responsibility to express caring for each other. Observe them, talk to them about how they preserve their commitment and work at building the same qualities into your own marriage.

✠ Build commitment by developing trust in each other

Cleaving, fusion, becoming and remaining committed — whichever term you choose, all necessitate trust. Trust is also needed when we leave the childhood/parent relationship. Normally, even though it does occur, we will not leave home with someone who is untrustworthy.

Trust is the foundational element for all healthy relationships. At the remaining-committed stage of the marriage, trust is needed at several levels. One basic indicator of the trust level in a relationship is the freedom to express an opinion, knowing you will not be criticised or condemned.

Yvonne and Jim were not very aware of each other's opinions on a great number of issues and were threatened when differences arose. Jim would feel rejected if Yvonne expressed a contrary opinion and Yvonne would then refrain from commenting for fear of offending Jim.

There were two taboo issues in Jim and Yvonne's home during those early years — in-laws and politics. Jim felt he had a good relationship with his in-laws if he saw them at Christmas and birthdays. His own parents were not very big on get-togethers, so it suited them fine. Yvonne, however, felt Jim was purposely avoiding her parents and became hurt very early when Jim said he didn't want to visit her folks so regularly. So in-laws weren't discussed and Yvonne felt offended.

Politics was Jim's area of 'expertise'. He knew for certain what deals were being made and which politicians were 'crooked' and so, when Yvonne would make statements based on TV commentary or magazine articles, Jim would become most indignant and discount her vocalised opinions — so in-laws and politics became taboo.

Neither felt free to discuss these topics because they seemed to result only in hurt and anger. Instead of feeling committed, they felt isolated. Feeling unsafe with each other in these areas, they found it harder to trust each other, even in other areas.

Trusting enough to be honest with our opinions and allowing our partner to do the same is vital if growth in commitment is to be experienced. Commitment does not mean sameness, but it does mean safety to express ourselves honestly and without fear of criticism.

Jim and Yvonne had trouble trusting each other with their opinions and this raises the issue of vulnerability. When we expose ourselves by sharing our opinions, beliefs, competence or emotions, we make ourselves vulnerable. We know we are taking a risk. We can be hurt if our partner ridicules us, ignores us or uses what we share against us at some future time. To share deeply about the intimacies of life takes trust. No-one wants to be exposed and then ridiculed or rejected — and so the temptation is to not share, not risk, but rather to become an emotional hermit. This is not the way to build intimacy. Trust means putting yourself at risk for the sake of genuine closeness by sharing with your partner. And it also means being trustworthy by handling as a precious gift whatever our spouse shares with us.

One major area in which trust functions — perhaps *the* major area — is fidelity. Partners cannot remain committed to each other unless they feel safe in the exclusivity of their relationship. The sexual unity of a marriage will be discussed fully in the next chapter, but it is important to note here that being unfaithful is incredibly destructive to a marriage relationship. It runs totally counter to this foundation of remaining committed. *No psychologically healthy person can trust someone they know to be unfaithful.* When a person trusts another with his or her sexuality, it is a sacred trust. To betray this by infidelity is to plant dynamite under the unity of the marriage.

✠ Build commitment by covenanting *to* each other

Our third component in the equation for cleaving is that the commitment we make needs to be centrally *to* each other.

When Jim and Yvonne made their wedding arrangements, they made sure the limousines were the correct make, the colour coordinators were on the job, the photographer was of the right school and so on. Most weddings are like that. We want the externals to be right.

Sadly, they didn't give as much attention to the most important aspect — the vows that they would make to each other. All too often, the most important aspect of the wedding is overlooked — the vows!

The vows are the central expression of our commitment to each other in marriage. When a husband and wife make their marriage vows to one another in the wedding ceremony they are, in effect, establishing a new covenant, a new agreement. The previous agreement in which they were primarily a member in their family of origin, with its roles, relationships and messages, is now being laid aside in order to establish the new.

The importance of this is signalled by the significant ways in which Western society established the marriage commitment. Traditionally (at least until we hit the age of watered-down vows), we required husband and wife to make a threefold vow. They pledged themselves:

* to each other
* before God
* in the presence of such witnesses as their family and friends.

Thus we sought to help ourselves; we attempted to dramatise the marriage for ourselves: 'This is really important. I really take this seriously. I will remain committed, for richer, for poorer, in sickness and in health, until death do us part. And God and my closest friends are witnesses that I have made these promises.'

To have this 'forever' attitude requires a great amount of tolerance, trust and determination. This determination is needed to work through the hard times when hurts are plentiful and the door seems to beckon. This determination is needed to see the relationship not just survive but blossom. It is as we give serious attention to building a fixed commitment into our marriage, that we actually engage the process of living out these vows.

Jim and Yvonne made hard going of this aspect of remaining committed. There were several times in the early years when Yvonne threatened to leave and return to her parents. Many couples take that option and the relationship never recovers. Sometimes it may be necessary for safety reasons to separate from an abusive spouse — and we support this when it is needed. But in many marriages, the reason for separating is not physical abuse and, in these situations, a determination to love and work through the hurt produces better results.

It seems that a committed relationship creates a security within us that breeds an intimacy level deeper than any other. We will expand on this concept later, but it is apparent that it works both for individuals and for couples.

✠ Build commitment by constant mutual reaffirmation

It is important to note that commitment should never be presented as a 'one time only' event. We need constantly to reaffirm our commitment to our spouses. This doesn't mean we have to retake our vows annually, although that might be a good thing, but it does mean we should let our spouses know regularly that we are remaining committed to them.

Be imaginative. You know your spouse! Find new ways to say, 'I'm recommitting myself to you because we belong together.'

As we have noted, the media's basic rip-off position is that lifelong commitment is impossible, unreal or perhaps not much fun. Don't you believe it! Sadly, also, they really have no concept of the depth of joy and intimacy that can be achieved when two people mutually care for each other, trust each other and remain committed to each other.

This commitment must be mutual; it must be the responsibility of both parties. It is so easy to leave the 'work' in a marriage to the 'more committed' partner. But the task is mutual; it is for both to work at.

One very important aspect of this mutual responsibility is that, as well as continually renewing *our* commitment, we seek also to help our partner to remain committed.

There are two ways a couple can encourage commitment in their spouse. The first way, emphasised by Dr Larry Crabb in *The Marriage Builder*, calls upon each person to set the goal of learning to serve his or her spouse, rather than manipulating. If I can set myself the lifelong goal of seeking to meet my wife's needs, rather than manipulating her by threats, tantrums, guilt or anything else, then I will provide her with a context of love that will make it so much easier for her to maintain her exclusive commitment to me for life.

The second way requires us to be constantly forgiving and seeking forgiveness to prevent the loss of communication and the erection of barriers. This we will take up further in a later chapter.

Be aware that, in order not to break faith with our wife (or husband), we have to guard ourselves. Society, particularly through the media, will bombard us with messages suggesting that it isn't important to remain committed. There are even 'experts' foolish enough to tell us that breaking our commitment can spice up our marriage. The message is wrong, but it is insistent, insidious and pervasive. We have to guard ourselves.

In effect, this means learning not to overdose on the media's value-diet. We actually will benefit by making decisions about what we view, read and absorb. Guard yourself in your thought life, in your fantasies. Guard yourself relationally. Don't let office friendships, or other relationships, develop to the point where they take the place of your primary relationship with your marriage partner. On that foundation, your marriage can go places!

In this chapter, we have noted the generally destructive role of the popular media, as it relates to the concept of remaining committted in marriage. We are unashamedly old-fashioned. We really have only one defence for pleading the importance of this position over that popularised in the media. Measured in terms of fulfilment in marriage, ours works; theirs doesn't!

But it is the third foundation to which we now turn our attention.

Questions for thought and discussion

✠ PERSONAL INVENTORY

Remaining committed can best be thought of as a fusion of two individuals into a functional unity. The actual process of fusion involves developing trust, accepting responsiblity for each other and a growing commitment to each other. In this chapter, we have seen how this process of fusion can be achieved.

The ideal situation would be for an engaged couple to be working on the process long before their wedding. This would mean the marriage would have a sound foundation so that when the 'leaving' occurs, the 'remaining committed' is emotionally and spiritually well under way. These few questions can be used for engaged couples or 'old' married couples alike:

1. What first attracted me to my spouse (fiancée/fiancé)?

2. I am doing the following three things to promote my spouse's welfare, growth and dignity:
   *
   *
   *

3. With whom/what is my spouse competing for my full devotion?

4. How do I react when my spouse expresses an opinion contrary to mine?
   I feel
   I say
   I act

5. When have I felt the closest to my spouse?

✠ SHARING WITH YOUR PARTNER

Ask your spouse to read your answers and you read theirs. Then share any answers that were unexpected and how they affected you upon reading.

Discuss whether there are any 'taboo' subjects between the two of you. List these and share the feelings these topics bring to the surface. You might consider these taboo subjects a gauge of trust in the relationship. What do you think?

Finally, recall those marriage vows and discuss how you're doing. Maybe you would like to take a week and rewrite them in your own words, then exchange them (in public or private) again.

✠ GROUP WORK

6. Have several members of the group share the most imaginative ways their spouse has expressed their commitment to them.

7. Try to compile a list of the various 'anniversaries' the members of the group have celebrated with their spouses. Have some share the more memorable ones.

8. Have the more mature couples share how they handled the hard times. This means vulnerability and acceptance are needed. Be prepared to process feelings as they arise.

9. Conclude by having several couples share what has helped to create 'fusion' in their marriage.

3

Become one by building 'coupleness'

IF LEAVING 'STUFF' IS THE FIRST FOUNDATION essential for getting a marriage off to a good start and remaining committed is the second, then ongoing attention to the task of becoming one or building 'coupleness', as distinct from singleness, is the third foundation. In this chapter, we want to explore the meaning of this phrase, to capture all that is involved in becoming one.

Becoming one obviously includes sexual union, but is a much bigger task than sexual union alone. If two different people are to become one, how is this 'oneness' achieved? Why is this 'oneness' important and where does it lead? We now take up these issues.

✠ Becoming one begins with a sense of mystery and wonder

For couples contemplating the wonderful time when they can fully share and express their love, there has always been a marvellous sense of wonder and mystery about marriage. Even just thinking about it can be exciting! Talking together and planning their future often evokes a sense of expectancy and delight. But it is that sense of mystery which is, most often, the greatest.

This sense of mystery and wonder is normally strong in every young couple embarking on the journey of marriage. As yet, they don't know what is fully in store and their imaginings will frequently be quite immature. But they sense that there are possibilities here — possibilities of richer and deeper experiences of love than they have ever previously known. That draws them on; that entices them; there is a promise of something that could be wonderful.

They are right. Marriage offers all these possibilities.

To have the joy of becoming 'one flesh' in marriage is for most couples wonder enough. To realise this means not only establishing their new relationship as husband and wife, but becoming a new — and unique — family! It is, existentially, quite immense to ponder the fact that, if they do this well, she will know him and he will know her at a level of reality deeper than any other person will ever know either of them.

What is so unique about marriage that it evokes this sense of wonder? Recognised or unrecognised, when we begin the journey of marriage, we move into new territory — territory that involves us in leaving aspects of singleness, while we learn aspects of functional unity in our coupleness. It is territory with a relatively unfamiliar vocabulary — intimacy, vulnerability, sacrificial love. It is territory with unfamiliar emphases on behaviours such as sharing, being unselfish, cooperating, compromising, thinking of our partner first.

Psychologist Erik Erikson pointed out that the central task of this period of life is the learning of intimacy skills in order to experience deeper levels of intimacy.

If we handle things well, we grow in our experience of intimacy; if we fail to handle things well, we experience deeper levels of physical and emotional isolation. Venturing deeper into intimacy is, for each of us, replete with wonder and mystery. So the task of becoming one is something that grips our hearts.

Of course, it is important to recognise that this sense of mystery and wonder is not the only dynamic working in us as we begin a marriage. Frequently, right alongside, right there on the surface, there is a sense of nagging doubt, fear and insecurity. It is important to acknowledge these, too, and we will take them up in more depth later in this chapter, but for now it is enough to note that they also exist, right alongside our magical hopes, and that their presence is fairly normal. Carrying some doubts in a marriage is not the kiss of death that some of us think it is.

It is great to have hopes, dreams and a sense of mystery and wonder in marriage. Unfortunately, they don't take us very far on the journey of deepening oneness!

✠ Becoming one requires working towards the goal of oneness

Entering into the mystery and wonder of marriage, of course, is only a beginning. Understanding the ideal of marriage is another important step in helping us move towards that goal of oneness.

Lovers who are learning to love need, really before marriage, to have clear goals about relationship and how to build it. Oftentimes, people don't understand the importance of the goal of developing their coupleness, let alone how to do this.

Take the case of Camilla and Ed. They had been married just a little over six years. She was a gifted communicator who had studied public relations and had held a good job with a city firm. He was a business major who had moved into management with a big accountancy firm, a job that required quite a bit of travel, long hours, frequent weekend work and lots of deadlines. They had met at university and had fallen in love.

Almost from the moment of their marriage, Camilla's unhappiness had begun. There never seemed to be enough time for them to talk, because Ed's job grabbed up all the spare time there was. Her attempts to beautify their home either went unnoticed or drew some muttered criticism. The fun things that they had done at university were a fading memory.

After four years of marriage, Camilla became pregnant and their son, Angus, was born. Camilla left her work to give time to mothering young Angus. She anticipated that it would improve things for her — that it would bring new meaning and fresh significance into their marriage. It didn't. She hoped Ed would get interested in his son and spend more time at home, relating in the family. He didn't.

When they came for their first counselling session, the marriage was in deep trouble. They were fighting and arguing more and more. Camilla was experiencing transient bouts of depression, during which she would simply let the house go. ('I hate housework anyway. Besides, he never appreciates anything I do.') Stress and pressure were building in Ed and he was becoming more verbally aggressive.

As I heard their story and watched them interact, a question began to form in my mind. Finally, I asked it. 'What was the date of your marriage again?' Camilla volunteered, 'The 19th of December.' She mentioned the year. 'You know, I think that's a big part of your problem,' I said. 'On that day, the 19th of December, I think both of you attended the wedding, but only one of you got married. I think both of you went through the wedding ceremony but, in a way, Ed stayed single. Could that possibly be the reason things started to go wrong?'

The non-verbal communication was a study in contrasting emotions. Camilla almost burst as she said, 'It's true; that's exactly what I think happened.' Ed was looking more puzzled, even a bit defensive. 'What do you mean?' he asked.

'Well, I think Camilla tried to adjust her life to the new situation of marriage. She wanted to reapportion her time and work at doing things together and so on. But it sounds like, because you didn't realise that you need to do those things to build a marriage, you didn't. It sounds like you basically kept doing much the same as before, when you were single — getting up, going to work, coming home, doing a bit more work, going to bed and so on. It sounds like your life didn't change much at all.

'Even when Angus was born, it sounds like you tried hard not to let the birth of a son change anything for you. Now I'm not reprimanding you — and this certainly isn't an issue of blame — but I'm trying to understand what's been going wrong for the two of you. Is it making any sense to you?'

Ed nodded assent and we went on. It turned out, not surprisingly, that Ed was following the model his father had set — work hard, get ahead, achievements are what count, be a good provider because that's what marriage is all about! As we talked about it, he could see that his parents' marriage was not a very good model. They were loyal to each other, but there didn't seem to be much intimacy. 'Sadly, I don't think your father ever got married,' I said.

Over the weeks, we focussed on a number of patterns of dysfunctional relating that had developed in Camilla as a result of hurt and loneliness, but much of our counselling centred around the question: 'What do we need to do this week to get Ed more married?' While his work situation made large changes difficult, we were able to chip away, increasing fun time together, getting communication going, involving Ed in more of the household happenings. Not long ago, two fairly happy people came to the conclusion that Ed was 'married now' and that it was 'pretty good', and that they didn't need to keep on with counselling any longer.

How can we grow in oneness?

First, we need to recognise the importance of a lifelong commitment to growing together. It simply will not happen unless we make it a goal and figure out, in practical terms, steps to take that will keep us moving towards the goal.

Like Ed, many people fail to recognise the importance of readjusting things when they marry. While they like the idea of being married, of having sexual and emotional needs met by a spouse and of feeling valued by that person, they don't so much like the idea of learning to set aside their own needs, preferences and wishes in order to acknolwedge and meet some of their spouse's.

Second, we need to make adjustments to the way we spent our time when we were still single. We have to recognise, and make concessions to, the needs of our partner — even though at times this will mean putting aside our own needs for the time being. When a child is born, we have to adjust our personal time schedule again. Having another person enter our family is no small thing, even if that person is just a baby. When the second child is born, we have to readjust again. Husbands and wives have to talk through the implications and willingly work together in order to get the most out of each new and enriching change.

So, being willing jointly to readjust the way we use our time and the relative priority we give to the activities that make up our lives are vital if we are going to move towards the goal of oneness.

Third, and most important, we need to undergird our marriage relationship with something we'd often rather not know about — unselfish love! To even talk about it as something integral to deepening intimacy is to risk a literary bullet in the back from some other writer. But honestly, haven't we just about had enough of so-called 'experts' who talk and write as though you can build a cosmic-experience marriage on a foundation of selfishness? The bottom line is, you can't!

How many individuals, in how many struggling marriages, over how many centuries of time, have searched for a decent alternative to, say, sharing, or giving in sometimes, or 'not having to do it my way'? There just aren't any decent alternatives. Demanding your own way, using aggressive tactics, bullying, scaring your partner into submission, manipulating, nagging, splattering your spouse with sarcasm, withholding affection, going silent — none of them work well for us.

It's hard for a wife to share herself at deeper levels of intimacy with a husband who regularly loses his temper, swears, breaks furniture and is abusive. And it's hard for a husband to share himself at deeper levels of closeness with a wife who is critical, never gives encouragement, manipulates and demands. We may, in the instance, get our own way, as if that's what life and marriage is all about, but the goal that our heart really longs for in terms of closeness, intimacy and oneness with the other simply moves further out into deep space.

Now, of course, this can all become a magnificent excuse for why we fail to do our part. 'Well, I would have,' you say 'but she's unlovable! No man could have loved her!' Or, 'Don't blame me. How could any wife respect a husband like him?' None of us is entitled to claim the luxury of these excuses. If we want the intimacy and wonder of oneness in our marriage, we have to get on with doing what will build it. It's time for us to adjust to the reality that there is no good alternative to unselfish love of our marriage partner. Anything less ends up being truly, and deeply, self-defeating.

Now the ramifications of this are big. Understood right, they mean that we have to love our spouse with, at least, the same love that we have for ourselves. Maybe, even more. You're right. It's scary territory!

But the incredible thing is that it works. Do your own little test. Ask yourself: 'Who is the happiest couple I know?' If they are truly fulfilled and happy in their marriage, you will just have identified a couple who have made some progress in learning to relate to each other from a foundation of unselfish love.

Or go the other way. Identify a couple whose marriage is struggling. Any sense of how good they are at living out unselfish love with each other? Convinced? The husband who neglects to work at loving his wife this way need never puzzle too long over why he and his wife don't seem to have grown very close or intimate. And the same truth exists for the wife. The miracle of oneness doesn't grow unless this requirement is being met.

We grow in becoming one with our spouse as we grow in learning to take our own selves off centre stage and putting our partner there. It is not by receiving things from our spouse in marriage, but rather by the giving of ourselves to him or her that we make our boldest moves towards the wonder of oneness.

Where both partners give themselves to doing it this way, there is a fusion of persons, but without the loss of self. Together, they begin to express themselves as a couple. They seem to be complementary. They exhibit a sense of wholeness, while each still retains his or her distinctiveness; they begin to taste the mystery and wonder of oneness!

✠ Becoming one means overcoming our fears

As we noted earlier, a sense of wonder is not the only thing we take into marriage. Usually, we also take our little (or big) bag of fears. Not surprisingly, people are often apprehenseive about this business of becoming one — and especially what they perceive to be the potential cost.

One of the important truths is that two people can begin to 'become one' without losing their individuality and distinctiveness. But, not infrequently, marriage partners become nervous about this as a possible hidden cost. Fearful of losing their individuality, they set themselves up to try to build a good marriage without doing the self-denying love bit. Not surprisingly, it doesn't work. Competitiveness often seems to replace oneness in these marriages.

The underlying assumption of the 'I'm going to look out for Number 1' approach to building a great marriage is that, if I can get my way all the time and never have to compromise or yield to the needs of my spouse, I'll be happy.

It's worth looking at where we ever got that idea.

Basically, we brought that one into the world with us. It is exactly the approach of the three-year-old who won't let any other child play with 'my toys', and who now sits lonely and isolated surrounded by all the toys, but with no friends! Of course, normally we wouldn't fall for it ourselves, but we have been engulfed with it just a little from the media over the past few decades. Lots of media presentations about the 'wealthy, the beautiful and the powerful' make it seem as though that's the way to go, folks, if it's real happiness and fulfilment you're a-seeking!

Sober reflection on common human experience

doesn't support the notion. How many active proponents of 'me first' watch as marriages crumble, friendships wither, loneliness gnaws and human and emotional vultures gather on the horizons of their life? It's time we assembled the evidence again and recognised that we don't have a whole lot to fear just because we've decided it's not important to 'have all the toys' in our marriage. We do not lose ourselves when we love another unselfishly. We create an environment in which we can the more truly experience dimensions of ourselves in intimacy. That, without such an experience, will always remain a longed-for dream.

How can we progress in giving to our spouse? Only if we have achieved a reasonable level of personal security. Low self-esteem and chronic self-doubt leave us so needy ourselves that we often seem unable to give to our spouse. Not infrequently, the holding back from oneness is a tacit admission that we are insecure in the depths of our being. Usually, this blockage requires counselling, so that people can work through things and move to deeper levels of self-acceptance.

Over the years, we have counselled many couples where one or other of the partners struggles for self-acceptance, with the result that they try to get all their needs met in their marriage relationship. Once again, because the emphasis is on getting rather than giving, the quest for genuine intimacy is a fruitless one.

But what happens to the couple where this journey towards oneness is not a part of the foundation for the marriage? Well, it certainly does not mean that the marriage is doomed. But it does probably indicate that, sooner or later, pressures both within and outside the marriage will find the couple without adequate resources to cope effectively.

Take the story of Mervyn and Lyn. I was counselling

them in one of their early sessions. 'Why does he get so angry? Can't Merv understand I'm often not ready to make love early in the morning when he wants to? Can you explain my needs to him?' Married more than thirty years and with a grown family, they were desperate to find answers and ways of recapturing something of the first love which their relationship had promised. Conflicts unresolved, poor communication and loss of intimacy — these were only the most obvious issues needing help.

At work, Mervyn was senior executive manager of his department. He believed he needed to keep on top of his job by aggressively not allowing anyone to get close. This kind of attitude also often pervaded his relationship with Lyn who also worked full time. Their frequent clashes resulted only in more barriers being erected between them.

When we looked together at the nature of their oneness, they soon discovered that, while they had some common goals, their oneness was more apparent than real. Both members of their local church, they did try sometimes to pray together, but they were not comfortable and at peace about this kind of intimate sharing. Also, both were still obviously too dependent for their happiness on the other's satisfaction of their personal needs.

And when either failed to come through for the other, a new clash would result, another barrier was erected. Little true intimacy and much ineffective communication meant the foundations of their relationship were crumbling. Little wonder then that Lyn's morning tiredness and frequent refusal to make love meant Mervyn was often sexually frustrated and angry.

The reality for Mervyn and Lyn was that they needed to recognise that they were largely operating in the marriage out of deep personal neediness and so were not able to make the effort to give to each other, putting self-centred operating aside. For both Mervyn and Lyn, it meant the painful task of acknowledging their neediness to one another, addressing the issues underlying this and seeking to establish again a priority of reaching out to each other to rebuild what had been lost in terms of oneness.

✠ Becoming one usually means becoming a family

In the course of preparing them for their forthcoming marriage, I often ask engaged couples: 'What are the most exciting things about being in love? What do you really look forward to in your marriage?' Most will then glowingly begin to speak about each other and their better qualities, the wedding, possibly their home, or even their future lives together. But few ever seem to talk about children or what is involved in becoming 'a family'.

Why is it, do you think, that this is so? Is it merely assumed, taken for granted, or is it, in these sophisticated times, an option to be considered later — a decision postponed until you can see if the relationship is working out well enough?

One of the strong marks of any society is the quality of its families. It is our contention that the moral and spiritual strength of families is directly related to the quality of oneness attained in the parents' marriage and, in turn, passed on to the children. The benefits of a lifelong journey towards oneness in marriage are there for the whole family, parents and children — indeed, for the extended family as well!

Children are the natural fruit of marriage. While for some couples, having their own children is not possible, for a few others, valid reasons may exist to choose not to have any. But these are exceptions. Children are normally seen as the beautiful and life-enriching fruit of oneness expressed in the sexual union of a husband and

wife. They are the living legacies, the tangible expression
of the 'becoming one' of two distinct lives joined together
in marriage. And where they have received, as a gift, the
benefits of their parents' commitment to oneness, a rich
cycle of sharing and caring flows in their midst.

Five years ago, we attended Michael's country wedding. We saw him more recently when he returned to
the city to attend a funeral. Today, his letter came, telling
us of his separation from Nita. 'We talked about where
we wanted our relationship to go. Last year, I had said I
would like to have a family within the next two years. . .
she told me she didn't want to have a family ever. . . Since
I could not sacrifice my life goals and she was not prepared
to change hers, we separated. . . '

We were saddened by his news, but not really surprised. My wife and I could not help but wonder why
this basic issue had not been canvassed before marriage.
We also wondered what other issues might lie beneath
their difficulties in reaching agreement on whether or not
to have children. Apparently, this difference did not seem
to divide them at first. But now, their differences in views
and values had become insurmountable. In such a vital
area as having a family, the whole viability of the relationship was challenged.

Marriage means becoming one. It means becoming
one not only physically, but spiritually, emotionally and
cognitively. This normally involves having children and
establishing a new family. The new family will be an
expression of the oneness that has emerged from the
coming together of two love-giving hearts.

Of course, the new family will be independent of
families of origin — or it should be. Certainly, there will
be many aspects of the new family which will express
aspects of the families of origin. The new family may
value education because the families of origin put a high

value on it. The new family may give their Christmas
gifts on Christmas Eve, rather than on Christmas Day,
because this tradition comes from one or both families of
origin. But it will also be different. At its best, as we
noted in chapter 1, the new family will also be an
expression that has left behind lessons, values, roles and
patterns of relating that are counter-productive. It will be
a new family. And this new family will also be a rich and
unique expression of the parents' becoming one.

But becoming a new family also implies developing the
kind of relational maturity appropriate to family life.
Why do we need to develop this so early? Because, if this
is in view when we first marry, our ways of relating will
include preparation for the eventual parenting role.

There is nothing calculated more to put strain on a
relationship than parenting children when you are not
prepared. Often have we heard these words from young
couples like Ken and Kay: 'It was when we had our first
baby we found out just how unprepared for parenthood
we were. It wasn't only that our sex-life lost out, but Ken
and I had to learn things we never knew about children;
disruptions to sleep and loss of our social life soon killed
our romance. I think that was when I first questioned my
love for Ken.'

It soon came out as we shared that they had not talked
much about their marriage beyond the wedding, nor had
they previously thought about family life, or adequately
prepared to become parents. They had not thought much
about the practical realities of becoming one at all, especially of how things would need to be readjusted as they
started a family.

Maturing love, if it is prepared early by true oneness,
however, will anticipate parental roles and other such
changes. These roles involve the provision of a special
place of nurturing for the wider family that will one day

come into being. 'If I had known then what I know now, I'd have prepared myself much better,' said Margaret to us recently. 'I don't think anyone can start too early to find out about what marriage and parenting is all about!'

Why is it that so few starry-eyed romantics are concerned much about the next year? If they think beyond the wedding, it is usually the house purchase and mortgage loan that receives their attention. Becoming materially secure often seems to displace the importance of growing towards oneness physically, emotionally, spiritually and relationally. Without this ongoing, significant commitment to move towards oneness, any marriage will find itself struggling for lack of substantial foundation.

As we have seen, if marriage is to become the fulfilled and happy experience hoped for, adequate thought and preparation towards laying this third and final foundation has to be made.

None will find building this foundation of oneness very easy. A few may be able to achieve it early in their marriage. But for many, like Camilla and Ed, there is the need to work hard, even seeking help towards building this basic foundation.

Others, like Mervyn and Lyn, need to overcome fears or other deep emotions to recapture the oneness they once had. Or you may identify with Ken and Kay, realising that complete oneness can only be fully learnt in the sacrifices and joys of parenthood.

At whatever stage your marriage may be, this goal of becoming one is the third foundation needed to build a mature and fulfilling marriage. But it needs to be recognised that it is a *lifelong* goal. If marriage is to retain the freshness and wonder which is such a feature of its beginnings, we must persevere in pursuing this goal. If we let things slide because 'our marriage is doing okay', we are risking the loss of the current level of marital satisfaction. It is hard to stand still in a marriage.

And one thing more. It is our conviction that true oneness in marriage has a spiritual dimension that many do not acknowlege or give much priority to. In some respects, this spiritual oneness may be the most important piece of oneness. For this reason, we encourage people to find a way to draw on the Reality who is God — to seek his help and share their experiences of him with each other — in their lifelong journey towards oneness.

Before leaving this section, we suggest that you take the time to work through the following questions and discuss them with your spouse. It will help you identify important aspects and indicators of work that you may still need to do on your marriage foundations. It will also prepare you for the work of building that we address in the next section.

Questions for thought and discussion

✠ PERSONAL INVENTORY

The special focus in Chapter 3 is on growing together as one. We must learn in marriage to think and act differently. It is here we learn to adjust to being *other-centred*: to become accustomed willingly to share in all life offers, and to learn the mystery and joy of becoming *one*.

We need to learn the true basis for love which will enable us to grow together in this oneness, so that a strong foundation for close intimacy is built. As relationships are strengthened and developed in love, any fears and uncertainties can be overcome.

Like everything else worth having, strong and lasting marriages require effort and thought. So it is important now to ponder a little and think about this particular foundational aspect of your marriage.

1. What uncertainties did you feel when you married?

2. In what ways have these uncertainties been partly, or completely, resolved?

3. To what extent did you readjust your life when you married? (Consider such areas as work, recreation, social life, time schedules and so on.)

4. On a scale of 1 (= almost none) to 10 (= constantly present) how much does 'unselfish love' show up in the way you relate to your spouse? Give yourself a score.

5. What changes could you make to increase the presence of 'unselfish love' in your way of relating to your spouse?

6. To what extent do you focus on your partner's imperfections and so hinder the process of building 'coupleness'?

7. What insecurities, or other blockages, have slowed your growth to marital oneness over the years?

8. What action could you take to help move you past some of the blockages?

9. What can you and your spouse do to strengthen your commitment to a life of growing deeper in your oneness?

✠ SHARING WITH YOUR PARTNER

Use the questions above as a stimulus for significant discussion and effective communication between you and your spouse. It will need time set side as a priority if the most benefit and positive change is to occur. This is something you can do for each other to provide a better foundation for your marriage.

List some steps you can take together to deepen your oneness — and plan to take action on them!

✠ GROUP WORK

10. Share in the group any special blessing that has come to your marriage as *oneness* has come.

11. What has helped you most in building your togetherness over the years of your marriage? Share in the group.

12. What have been the biggest blockages to deepening intimacy in your marriage? Ask the group's ideas on moving ahead through these.

13. Have couples identify and share the times and activities in marriage which have been special times of closeness. Use these ideas to generate a wider pool of possibilities for *your* marriage.

14. Those in the group with children could share their experiences:
    a. How has parenthood impacted growth of oneness?
    b. How has having children contributed positively over time in building 'coupleness'?

Part B:
Building

4

Have realistic expectations

ONCE THE FOUNDATIONS OF A HOUSE HAVE BEEN laid, the building can get under way. So it is with marriage. With the foundations in place, inspected and approved, the work of putting an enduring, fulfilling marriage on those foundations can begin.

But there are certain things to watch out for. In this chapter, we set out to understand some of what we might call the big disappointments that get in the road of good construction. By recognising and guarding against these, we can prepare ourselves more realistically for the work of strong marriage-building. Some of these disappointments happen because we start with unrealistic expectations.

✠ Big Disappointment #1:
'But it's hard work!'
In some respects, nothing could set us on the track of unrealistic expectations for marriage more than the wedding! It is such a starry-eyed day.

You know the scene. The groom is finally organised and, along with a couple of close friends, has rented a double-breasted, grey Al Capone suit! These suits are two sizes too big, except for the best man's which combines a coat with sleeves coming halfway down his hairy forearms with a pair of trousers that have the cuffs rolled up three times. Two vintage Jaguars from a friend's uncle's next-door neighbour have been rented to transport the bridal party. The Jaguars make a nice contrast with the rusty VW Beetle that they plan to use to drive away in for the honeymoon.

The bride looks, shall we say, stunning, in her Igor Stravinsky, IBM-compatible, user-friendly bridal gown, complete with organza veil and three-metre train. The bridesmaids, in their lemon chiffon dresses with tartan stockings, draw impressive gasps from the onlookers. The ceremony, a monument to creativity, will live forever in the minds of the spectators, all fully recorded on VHS!

No expense has been spared on the wedding banquet. Not the usual rubber chicken, but turkey with cranberry sauce! (To be honest, still just a little rubbery. . .) Everyone has wined and dined elegantly and so the couple head off for the honeymoon — two weeks at Nirvana Beach.

Often there is not a lot of reality to these days, but they well may bring an expectation that this is what married life is all about — excitement, spending money, having fun, relaxing in beautiful surroundings, minimal responsibility.

The trouble with this kind of scene is that it just can't last. Jobs, bills, weariness, sickness, competing wants, different ways of doing things, arguments, housework, children — all these and more intrude into our reality, causing us to wonder if we've been cheated somehow. How come it was so wonderful a little while ago and now it's such hard work? The truth is that married life is like any other part of life. It has its hard times as well as its good times. Some days, you'd just like to press the 'delete' button.

But that doesn't mean that marriage is not worth it. On the contrary, anything worthwhile takes effort and costs something. We need to know on the front end that, no, it will not always be the way the wedding and the honeymoon might lead us to expect. We need to know that, yes, we will have to work at it. We will have to learn to sacrifice some of our dreams. We will have to adjust and change.

Isn't it funny how we know the truth of this in other areas of life, but we hope to avoid it in the area of marriage? We know that we have to work hard to save the money for our block of land or to pay off the mortgage on our house. We know that we will have to slog away at the books to complete our work qualifications. And, most of the time, we can apply ourselves in these areas, because the goal is worthwhile.

Anything worthwhile takes effort and costs something. And marriage is definitely in this category. It is worthwhile. There are few things as worthwhile as a fulfilling marriage. But we need to be prepared to face the truth that there will be times of hard work along with the richness of fulfilment.

✠ Big Disappointment #2:
'My spouse isn't meeting all my needs'
Many different psychologists have attempted to categorise the needs that people have. Almost certainly the best-known is Abraham Maslow, whose hierarchy of human needs has been fertile ground for much research and theorising about human functioning.

Maslow suggested that there were five levels of human need ranging from the most basic, physiological needs such as food and water, through safety needs, love needs, esteem needs and, finally, self-actualisation. Certainly, all of these make sense as we think of ourselves.

It is true that I need my basic physiological demands to be satisfied. I need food and drink. I need warmth and shelter. I also need security, comfort and stability, if not all the time then at least some of the time; otherwise, I will be overwhelmed with the hardness of life. It is also true that I need my love requirements to be met. I need someone or some people to enable me to feel that I belong, that I am loved, that I am acceptable. We would also have no argument about the fact that I need to feel good about myself, to have a sense of positive self-worth. Without this, I will tend to be depressed and negative.

Lastly, we recognise that I need to move towards my potential, to have a healthy growing sense of self-awareness. Without this, I will be bored, alienated and unfulfilled.

Clearly, my marriage partner can never meet all of these needs. Yet, all too frequently, this unspoken assumption seems to be part of one or the other person's expectation of marriage and, when it is not met, it becomes a big disappointment.

James and Delia were a couple who had not rushed into marriage. They had worked together in a large company for a number of years and felt that they knew each other well when they finally decided to marry. When they came to see me, the marriage was tottering, even though there were now two young children. Delia was depressed and struggling to function. An assessment gave no family history of depression and no previous history for Delia. The evidence suggested that this was a reactive depression, caused by the quality of the relationship and the marked deterioration in it.

As we talked in that first session, Delia made a significant statement: 'And I always thought that I'd marry a knight in shining armour.' As we talked further about that statement, it became apparent that Delia would not forgive James for not meeting her need for such a 'knight'. His personality practically made it impossible, but she wanted him to be one and, since he wasn't, she had gradually built up anger at him.

Not surprisingly, the gradual accumulation of anger in Delia led to a significant decrease in the quantity and quality of their sexual relationship and also in their communication and general satisfaction with each other. James began to spend more time playing competition squash and practised several times a week — and that, of course, gave Delia more grounds for anger. Her 'knight in shining armour' had ditched her for a little rubber ball and the opportunity to sweat!

The separation cycle was under way. And, underneath it all, one of the key issues was that James had failed to meet what Delia perceived to be a priority need for her.

Certainly, in marriage our spouse can, and should, meet some of our needs. But he or she can never meet all of them. We need honestly to face human limitations and not expect *all* of our needs to be met in a spouse.

Some of our deepest needs will only be met in God. The search for inner spiritual peace, common to all people, will only be finally met as we relate to One who is beyond and above us. We can fall into the trap of trying to make our spouse fill the 'God-void' in our hearts, but finally any such attempt must fail. This is a need no spouse can meet. He or she can encourage and help us, but ultimately this need will only be met as we give time and energy to it ourselves.

Lots of people don't want to acknowledge the reality of their spiritual need. It's not 'cool'. 'If I can't touch it, or see it, it doesn't exist!' Spiritual realities thus get dismissed. Unfortunately, they don't go away so easily. What is real won't simply disappear because we deny its existence. In a thousand ways, the inner emptiness that is our soul's cry for knowing God keeps disturbing us. And we can never meet *that* need in a spouse!

Other needs will only be met in deep friendships with

people of our same sex — friends that a husband can share with in areas that are not of interest to his wife or girlfriends that a wife can share with in areas that are not of interest to her husband.

While much — even most — of our friendship needs can be met in a spouse, not all can. Nor should we try to force this. While my wife and I share a deep friendship, she simply is not very interested in my passion for body-surfing or watching the occasional late-night Rugby test. These are interest areas that I share more with my two sons and one or two close male friends. And that is good. The only danger would be if their friendship became, overall, more important to me than hers. Or if I spent more time with them than with her. But in its proper place, the friendship of others apart from our spouse is a gift to help meet some of our needs.

In all of this, we need to avoid using this truth as an excuse for not working to meet most of the needs of our spouse. Human nature being what it is, sometimes people latch onto something like this and use it to justify the failure to express love and unselfish caring for their spouse.

One of our life-tasks in marriage is to work to get the balance right. We will give ourselves as fully as we can to meeting the needs of our spouse. But we will also recognise our limitations and our spouse's limitations and not chafe under impossible expectations. If we get the balance right, we will not experience the big disappointment of feeling that our partner has let us down by failing to meet all of our needs.

✠ **Big Disappointment #3:**
   'But my husband/wife has changed. . .'
Sometimes, following the wedding, we begin to encounter irritating aspects of our marriage partner that were not so evident during the courting days. Unfortunately, courting

days are often filled with a tendency to see things through rose-coloured glasses. The same unreality that pervades the wedding and the honeymoon causes us to overlook troublesome aspects of our partner's personality and functioning. We frequently live with a degree of denial.

So the first thing that can be said about this disappointment is that it may not truly be a change in our spouse. It may simply be that now the rose-coloured glasses are off and we are seeing more clearly aspects of our partner that we didn't notice before. Suddenly, we see that our husband has an annoying tendency to sniff or we discover that our wife has an irritating habit of picking the skin off her heels when she reads books in bed! Why can't he or she be 'nice' like they were before we discovered this trait?

The solution to this problem lies in facing the truth that, in this instance, our partner has not changed. It is simply that, now that we live together, we see more clearly one another's peculiarities and annoying qualities. Now we see that we had an over-idealised picture of our spouse.

Part of the journey of building love is to discover how to love even the warts that we bring to our marriage. When we are talking about human beings, imperfection goes with the territory. A central part of our life adjustment when we marry lies in accepting that reality. If we cannot accept our spouse's imperfections, if we insist on choosing to criticise, to correct and pull down, we will never build love.

We need to see that it is children who *must* have things their way. Mature adults can find pleasure and fulfilment in the midst of imperfection, because that is the reality they live in. Accept your spouse. *Love the lovable and don't make a fuss of the imperfect.* None of us has it all right. It helps a lot to remind ourselves that we bring a few warts ourselves into the marriage!

But, at other times, the truth may be that our partner

has changed. These changes need not be disastrous, but they may signal a downward spiral in the quality of the marriage relationship and to that extent they are of concern.

Gina and Frank came with just such a story. Gina was ready to quit the marriage. Over the five years of the marriage, she had always tended to give more than Frank, but things had continued to slide. When she gave him an ultimatum, he finally came with her to seek counselling. He really didn't want to lose her. The history of their courtship and marriage revealed that Frank had actually won Gina's heart by pursuing her with little gifts of love. He would turn up at the office where she worked and drive her home; he would bring her a bar of chocolate and a rose. Over a long period of time, he won her heart.

The problem was that almost as soon as they were married, Frank stopped. He worked long hours and he used that as an excuse to become demanding and justify his failure to do anything loving for Gina now that they were married. Not surprisingly, the model of a husband passed on to him from his father was an incredibly dysfunctional one. His father had been a brutal dictator in the home. Frank was not brutal, but he certainly didn't know much about maintaining and building love. And Gina's growing anger had a real basis. He *had* changed.

As we talked through this concern, it became apparent that other problems existed. Communication had decreased and there was by now little enjoyment in the marriage. Although both had a number of issues to address, Frank was the one who had to begin. He had to put aside his selfishness and begin once again to show Gina some evidence of his love.

Changes like these need to be recognised and worked through. If they are denied or avoided, there is a real danger that hurts and resentments will build to a point where the marriage may not survive.

Sometimes, the changes that occur are very serious and damaging. He has developed a drinking problem or she spends more time with her girlfriends than with him. Sometimes, the reality is harsher still. He has become violent; she has been unfaithful.

There is no simple answer to problems as difficult as these. These are more than big disappointments. They are lethal weapons of destruction. Left unattended, they will rapidly destroy any marriage. In chapter 8, we explore some of the key issues associated with good management of anger in marriage.

At this point, it is perhaps enough to say that changes as significant as these may well be symptoms of other underlying problems, but something needs to be done quickly. Problems such as these almost certainly will require help from a trained counsellor if they are to be worked through by the couple.

✠ Big Disappointment #4:
'I'm carrying most of the load. . .'
When one partner in a marriage believes that he or she is doing most of the work to make the marriage function, this can put strains on the relationship.

Jeffrey was a competent, reliable employee, working for his company's sales staff. Six years earlier, he had married Lucy after a two-year courtship. Lucy had seen me as a client prior to their meeting and getting married. At that time, Lucy had suffered from a generalised anxiety disorder which we had traced back to some childhood experiences and to the modelling effect of a very anxious father. She had made good progress but, every now and then, cycled back into a period of not coping well. At these times, she would become excessively anxious about the health of her parents, her husband and child and would find it very difficult to cope at work. She would become preoccupied with worrying about everything and Jeffrey would have to pick up the load.

Jeffrey had made this appointment on his own. He confided: 'I need your help. I can see what's happening. I feel like I'm carrying most of the load in our marriage. I think I'm doing seventy-five per cent or more — and I'm starting to resent it. I know I'm starting to feel angry towards Lucy and I'm not talking to her so easily. I'm holding myself back. I'm under stress at work, but I don't feel like I can talk about that with Lucy — she wouldn't cope. I have to support her all the time, but she can't support me.'

It was not hard to sympathise with Jeffrey. By any objective standards, he had to carry most of the load — he had to be strong. Although she had made some progress, Lucy still functioned as a very dependent partner much of the time.

There is a reality to this kind of situation that needs to be addressed. First of all, the 'load-carrier' may need additional support. This is often the case when one partner in the marriage has a chronic medical problem that hinders him or her from functioning well. Or it may happen, as in this case, when one partner has an emotional problem that prevents healthy functioning. In situations like this, it is important for family or friends to become part of a support team, so that the load-bearer is able to have occasional breaks.

But just as important is the need for the load-bearer to receive help with his or her attitude. Frequently, as happened with Jeffrey, resentment begins to build and, over time, this can destroy the marriage. So one of the central tasks in this situation is for the load-bearer to deal regularly and ruthlessly with the resentment. Resentment is an emotional and spiritual issue. At the centre of our being we need to deal with resentment by handing it over to God and asking for help so that it doesn't overwhelm us. Left unattended, it can quickly kill love.

Resentment breeds criticism and coldness and anyone already struggling in their physical or emotional health will not be helped in their coping if they are regularly criticised, rejected and avoided. Clearly, affirmation and support provide more fertile soil from which improvements in health and emotional functioning can grow. So resentment has to be released to God every time it appears, so strength for each day can be provided.

We need to find ways of viewing the situation differently so that we are not focussing on the 'it's not fair' aspects of the relationship. We need to focus, instead, on the gifts, opportunities and privileges that await us in a situation where we can give more than our spouse.

Of course, all of this does not provide a blank cheque for the other partner to enjoy being the non-coper. We are all required in life to move towards full maturity, and this involves learning to handle our physical and emotional struggles without rushing towards dependence. It involves a never-ending commitment to the task of growing up. There are times when people adopt a life position of being a non-coper because it brings the benefit of being looked after by others. Whenever this occurs, it is always a tragic misdirection of life — a sad waste of the potential that exists in a person.

For Jeffrey, the task primarily involved handing over the build-up of resentment (sharing it with another person was a good start!), and this he did. He went away with a new focus — he was no longer preoccupied with the disappointment that he had to give more than fifty per cent in the marriage, but rather worked at identifying positive aspects of the marriage that he could give more air-play to.

He was able to identify quite a number of positives in his marriage. He was able to be thankful that his emotional health was secure and he was able to see that in many ways it was a privilege to be able to *give* to his wife. He had re-sorted some priorities, so that he would be able to get additional practical support if and when he felt the need for it. And he went with a new determination to give affirmation and love to Lucy.

✠ What about other disappointments?

The truth is there is almost an endless number of disappointments that people encounter in marriage. Some say that they are lonely, even after years of marriage. Some seem unable to handle the curtailment of personal freedom to do 'what I want to do'. And so the list goes on.

Without exception, handling these or our own special big disappointments well will require an adjustment in our perspective. We will need to make the central focus of our minds not what we are missing, but what we have gained. We will need to develop a perspective that rejoices in the many positives instead of focussing on the disappointments. The truth is, because humans are always imperfect, marriage will always have some deficits, some disappointments. We need to take that as a given and not be surprised, or unduly disturbed, when we discover some of these.

But the privileges of intimacy, the special joys of a covenant relationship of love with a marriage partner are immense. By committing ourselves to the joyful task of being givers of love to our marriage partner, by giving time to each other, learning to communicate deeply and affirmingly, we open ourselves to receive a harvest of benefits prepared for us in the master plan for meeting human intimacy needs.

Questions for thought and discussion

✠ PERSONAL INVENTORY

This chapter brings to the forefront our very human tendency to find the downside, even of things that are good. Part of us longs for novelty and variety so that even something which we initially find wonderful can easily start to seem pale and unsatisfying after a while. And then we start to see the faults, the disappointments. . .

Marriage is no exception. We usually have very little worthwhile preparation for this event which involves lifelong commitment. We are not at all used to lifelong commitment. Nothing else has been quite like this.

Our lack of good preparation shows up in unrealistic expectations. When the earliest flush of wonder is gone, it is easy to find ourselves honing in on the disappointments, getting preoccupied with things that 'aren't the way we thought they'd be' in the marriage. And an out-of-whack emphasis on these areas can quickly put a marriage in deep trouble.

1. What were three of my expectations about marriage and/or my marriage partner that I brought with me into my marriage?

2. Using a rating scale from 1 (very low) to 10 (very high), how would I rate the degree to which each of these expectations has been met in my marriage?

3. [For any scores below 5] What reasons can I give for the failure of my expectations to be met at a higher level in my marriage?

4. What has been the single most disappointing aspect of my marriage?

5. Have I shared this with my spouse? Why or why not?

6. If I shared it, how did I share it? How was it received?

7. What have I done about handling this? Building from the teaching in this book, what more can I do?

8. What is one area in which I know I've disappointed my spouse in our marriage?

9. What could I do to make his/her disappointment in this area less of an issue in our marriage?

✠ SHARING WITH YOUR PARTNER

Set a time when you and your spouse will discuss the issues raised by the personal inventory questions.

Once again, remind yourself of the key elements of good communication prior to sharing, so that you make this a positive communication experience. Keep your voice tone sensitive and loving, set your heart on *not* being offended, listen to each other and concentrate on understanding.

Discuss together any changes that could be made by either one of you, or by both, so that any disappointments are helped to fade into unimportance. Recognise that significant changes usually start in small ways, so don't plan to make dramatic changes immediately. Begin with small steps and discuss how you will support each other.

✠ GROUP WORK

[Answer these first questions in sub-groups of husbands and wives. Plan to give no more than one-third of the group time to this.]

10. Share with other group members one expectation that became a disappointment in your marriage.

11. Share with each other about the things that have helped you handle the disappointments. Be as specific as you can.

[In the combined group of husbands and wives:]

12. Share with each other the most helpful thing that you got out of this chapter.

13. Discuss any specific lessons from some other source that have helped you have a healthy and realistic understanding of marriage.

14. Discuss one aspect of your marriage that has given you a great deal of fulfilment and joy.

5

Cultivate loving intimacy

INTIMACY. THE WORD ITSELF CONJURES UP a host of different meanings to different people. We are all familiar with the word's use in the field of advertising — we hear of the 'intimate boutique' or the 'intimate lounge setting'. Both of these usages imply 'small and in close quarters', projecting an image of rubbing shoulders or physical closeness and the meeting of personal tastes.

We also find the word used to describe merchandise from the department store or the supermarket. We know of 'intimate apparel' such as lingerie and other 'intimate' items such as perfumes. These, too, portray a sense of personalised need and imply a sense of privacy, even mystery.

Each of these merchandising 'intimacies' does contain some similarities with the intimacy we speak of as being important in building a fulfilling marriage, but it is just a sliver. The sense of the personal and private is important, but there is more, far more.

But before we go any further, let's recognise one problem associated with this word. Intimacy is not a word with which males easily identify. The typical adult male thinks of intimacy as either sexual relating or 'women's talk'. Men aren't intimate; they're 'mates' or 'buddies' or, if pressed, 'close'.

It's a pity the word hasn't had a better PR program

directed at men because they have exactly the same needs for intimacy as do women. Unfortunately, often they don't recognise it.

Well, we acknowledge intimacy is misused and misunderstood, but what is it? Various attempts have been made to define intimacy. They usually include the concepts of connectedness and trust, of loving, special closeness. These aspects are central to the meaning of intimacy. That is what we really want out of marriage. We want to feel that we are in a relationship of special, loving closeness, where we care deeply for the other person and they care deeply for us. We want to feel that there is a special quality of trust and connectedness between us.

However, for our purposes, the emphasis we want to place upon intimacy involves expanding upon the concept of intimate knowing. Intimate knowing of another person involves a sense of knowing and, at the same time, loving and accepting them.

Intimacy, in this sense, is central in the building of marriages. We need knowledge of, and respect for, ourself and a knowledge and deep loving acceptance of our partner, to whom we are committed. The marriage relationship, among all human relationships, offers probably the best opportunity to develop true intimacy.

There are several important aspects of intimacy with which we need to acquaint ourselves if we are really going to unpack its meaning. These are:

1. a knowledge and commitment to growing yourself;
2. a knowledge and commitment to accepting your partner;
3. a commitment to giving and receiving love within the marriage.

If both husband and wife are committed to these aspects of intimacy, then intimacy can grow. The couple can begin to experience a freedom with each other, a personal knowing and acceptance of each other and a safety with each other. They have no shame, no barriers, about themselves or each other.

Unfortunately, this isn't true in many marriages. The more common story is that there are barriers, there are blockages. Freedom and safety with each other have not always been built in.

✠ Intimacy means knowing and growing yourself

Bill was a young executive who had been struggling with relationships for years. He was known as a loner and very few of his workmates counted him among their friends. Bill spent most of his spare time doing courses at college or tech. Underneath his 'I'm sufficient' exterior, Bill felt unworthy and inadequate in most areas. He studied to gain some sense of accomplishment, but couldn't face the uncertainty of risking relationships.

It wasn't until Bill took himself to counselling and worked through poor parental relationships and his fear of rejection that he accepted he could be a friend to someone and began to let people into his world.

Bill is typical of some who have a limited respect for themselves and very little understanding of their strengths and weaknesses. As it turned out, Bill was a very accomplished photographer. Most of his courses were media-related and he was able to join a small interest group at his church and begin to see his photographic skills as a positive attribute in his life.

Without acceptance of his own worth and valuing of his talents, Bill could not risk any vulnerability with anyone. And he could not undertake the journey of growing himself emotionally, spiritually and relationally. He was trapped in isolation.

There are some people who have a poor self-image and yet value and respect others and are open to them. These people tend to be candidates for abusive relationships. They idealise others at their own expense and open themselves in the vain hope that they will be accepted because of their vulnerability. These are not emotionally healthy persons. Often, they will become resentful and angry on the inside because they never feel truly valued in their relationships. They, too, miss out on intimacy. People such as these are co-dependent persons — they 'love too much' for their own good.

Sally was such a person. She had experienced limited love as a child and grew up starved of affection. As a child, she always tried to please and was almost embarrassingly compliant and willing. She only 'felt' loved when others gave her their approval. Unlike Bill, Sally was too open and was hurt badly by several relationships and an office manager who capitalised on her reluctance to trouble anyone else. Sally was trapped by co-dependency.

Neither Bill nor Sally could experience real intimacy. Bill had missed out because he excluded everyone from his world. Sally missed out because she couldn't include herself among the acceptable people in her world.

Real intimacy is built upon knowing ourselves and being able to affirm and accept ourselves, even with our faults and imperfections. Of course, this doesn't imply that we have the freedom to sit back and not work on our faults, but certainly it is never easy to work on personal shortcomings if we reject ourselves at a deep, fundamental level. We need to know ourselves and accept ourselves as part of the journey of building intimacy. And we need to continue the journey of growing ourselves in understanding, in emotional maturity, in healthy relational skills and in spirituality right throughout our adult lives.

✠ Intimacy means knowing and accepting your partner

A second dimension of intimacy involves knowing and accepting your partner, even with his or her faults and imperfections. It is fundamental to our growing in knowledge and acceptance of our partner for us to begin from a position of accepting the equal value of males and females. Nothing is more destructive to the development of intimacy than to have one person (usually the male) assume, and live out of, a position of superiority. True, there are functional differences but, in terms of worth and personhood, male and female are equal.

In any intimate relationship, the participants hold the needs and desires of the other in utmost regard. To ignore or abuse the needs and desires of your partner can put the whole marriage relationship in jeopardy.

Take the case of Sandy. She was a high-need person. She was sensitive and gentle, her highest need being security. Her background had not provided this essential in her life and her husband, Joel, had been her main source. Over the past few years, Joel's work had removed him from the home for lengthy periods at a time. When he was home, Sandy became angry and upset over little things he did. She didn't know why but, as her security came and went, she became very anxious and resented the uncertainty. Joel in turn didn't understand her needs and took the mood changes as rejection. As a result, he pulled further away.

When Joel came to see his role in the behaviour pattern, he began to work on assuring Sandy of his commitment and his desire to be with her. He rearranged his schedule as best he could and called more often when away. Sandy in turn sought help in dealing with her many security-based needs and focussed on taking a more active role in meeting those needs herself. When these two people began to respect the needs they saw in each other, they began to regain the intimacy they had seen slip away.

✠ Intimacy means commitment to give and receive

The final aspect of intimacy is commitment. We have dealt with this dimension somewhat in chapter 2, but here we examine another aspect of commitment as it relates to the building of intimacy.

Intimacy as a loving commitment is not necessarily the passionate sexual love at times associated with intimacy, but the multi-dimensional love which all of us have a need for. We won't neglect the sexual side of intimacy. In fact, we will devote the whole of the next chapter to this important topic, but for now we want to focus on non-sexual loving intimacy.

The Greeks had several words to express the word 'love'. Whereas in English we use the word 'love' to cover many different aspects, the Greek language had a richer vocabulary and had several words from which to choose. Each of these words picks up on a particular facet of love. When these facets of love are combined, we have a fullness of intimacy varying from deep desire, through friendship, to sexual union.

The first of the non-sexual dimensions involves our imagination, our dreams and desires. The Greek word is *'epithumia'*. This is a strong desire, an overwhelming urge to be with someone. It can be inappropriately directed and be manifested as lust, or appropriately directed and be manifested as deep desire.

True intimacy involves aspects of *epithumia*. Husbands and wives need to desire to be with each other. The strong desires are the kindling that brings on the slow burn of passion that *epithumia* also encompasses. We all need to cultivate *epithumia*. This may involve thinking about our spouse in romantic ways, such as planning special events and occasions. It will involve creating mindmoods that set the scene for special times together or for physical intimacy.

To cultivate a deep desire to be with our spouse is to pick up on one of the beautiful facets of the diamond of intimacy.

Another form of love that contributes to intimacy is that of cherished affection, or what we might call friendship. The word used by the Greeks is *'philo'* — the sort of love that close friends share. It is the root word behind Philadelphia, the city of brotherly love. *Philo* love is a deep sense of caring that involves an emotional attachment whereby another's welfare is of major concern.

This dimension of loving intimacy is difficult for many men to get a handle on. Men are often not well prepared, culturally, for the task of sharing close thoughts and feelings with a wife. Women frequently share from adolescence with close girlfriends, but too often their male counterparts are active 'doing things' without any deep sharing. They would like the same level of closeness, but social taboo somehow forbids it.

In marriage, this can become a thorny issue, as wives expect their husbands to fill the role that girlfriends played and provide the close, sharing friendship of *philo*. Making progress in acquiring this form can prove quite a task for many men. However, the rewards are worth it. A couple who can cultivate this form of commitment share an intimacy that is longlasting and rewarding.

A further aspect of love that contributes to commitment is the love expressed in the Greek word '*storge*'. What a wonderful picture this word expresses. It has as its basis the sense of belonging to a family, the love that creates security and comfort. Every couple needs this form of intimacy where they know their downside will be accepted, where their faults will not be judged and where their pain will be shared. *Storge* is the 'I belong to you' intimacy that weathers any storm.

These emotional and psychological aspects of intimacy are complemented in the Greek language with the romantic/erotic love depicted in the word '*eros*'. This aspect of intimacy refers to the sexual/physical love discussed in the next chapter.

A final facet of love-committed intimacy is the spiritually-active component referred to by the Greek word '*agape*'. This love is the unconditional, sacrificial love that we are called upon to have in relation to our spouse in marriage. It might be thought of as an unconquerable benevolence towards our marriage partner. This love is active. It has an emotional dimension, but is not bound by emotion; it is, rather, a matter of the will.

A couple with this active love in their relationship will experience intimacy at its most rewarding. By activating our will to put the needs of our spouse above our own needs without an expectation of any return, we transcend the selfish aspects of common relationships and join in a gracious and truly loving intimacy.

✠ Barriers to intimacy

If knowing and accepting yourself and knowing and accepting your spouse are key ingredients to the development of intimate relationship, then it stands to reason that a major barrier to intimacy is the absence of such knowledge and acceptance. Sadly, in our clinics we frequently see couples who lack intimacy because one or both partners are ignorant of their own inner dynamics — the patterns of behaviour and the reasons they do these things. Even more sadly, sometimes we encounter people who are so threatened by the call to deeper self-knowledge and the call to knowing their partner at a deeper level that they do everything to avoid these tasks. They blame, they avoid, they deny — they find a hundred different ways of running.

The avoidance techniques vary, but the outcome is always the same — less intimacy! If we truly desire intimacy, we have no good alternative but to be committed to a lifelong journey of learning about ourselves — our idiosyncracies and peculiarities, our patterns of thinking, feeling and doing, our strengths and resources, our blind spots — in fact, everything that goes to make us the unique person we are. And we must pursue the same journey as it relates to understanding and accepting our marriage partner.

Tina and Perry presented for counselling because their sexual relationship was unfulfilling. For Tina, making love was frequently painful, so she had no great desire to share in this aspect of marriage with her husband. For Perry, there just was not enough love-making. It seemed a fairly simple issue — she had a problem; he was fine.

Of course, it was a little more complex. The truth was that Perry came from a family where his father had been waited on for all his needs by a doting (subservient?) wife — and a grandmother as well. In the marriage with Tina, he was contributing very little apart from going to work. The fact that Tina also worked didn't seem to make much difference.

As some of the underlying hurts in Tina began to surface, Perry pulled out of counselling. Tina still came to the next session, reporting that Perry 'didn't want to talk about all that other stuff'. He just wanted Tina to 'get fixed with her problem'. He didn't realise it, but he was settling for a marriage with diminishing intimacy. It was too threatening for him to make the journey towards understanding and growing himself and understanding and accepting his wife better.

The other major blockage is, of course, the failure to be committed to the giving and receiving of love in marriage. Unfortunately some people, because of their upbringing and the choices they have made through life, have little understanding of the many facets of love that exist. Usually, where this is the case, they only know of sexual love. Inevitably, the marriage becomes a sexual disappointment, because sexual love does not thrive in a context where there is no non-sexual love to complement it.

Sexual love is the theme of our next chapter. . .

Questions for thought and discussion

✠ PERSONAL INVENTORY

Intimacy is an essential ingredient for a truly fulfilling marriage. For the majority of females, it is a further development of the closeness they experienced in their single, same-sex relationships. For the majority of males, however, even the word is foreign.

To the typical male, intimacy equals sex. This is unfortunate, as it limits the depth of relationship available. The joy of experiencing intimacy in all its dimensions begins with a sound understanding of those dimensions including, but not restricted to, the sexual. So, let's explore this most elusive, but essential quality of relation-ship.

1. A knowledge and commitment to growing yourself is the initial aspect mentioned in working through intimacy. Make a list of the more obvious charac-ter strengths and weaknesses you are aware of in yourself.

Strengths	Weaknesses

2. What could you do to better utilise your character strengths to meet the needs of your spouse?

3. What are the ways you could improve your weaker character traits so as to be more able to enjoy intimacy?

4. In this chapter, Bill and Sally represent two differ-ing types of intimacy-missers. Which of the two more closely resembles you and why?

5. Which of the various facets of love do you find most difficulty relating to? What could you do to improve the situation?

✠ SHARING WITH YOUR PARTNER

6. From the section 'Intimacy means knowing and accepting your partner', have one of you read Sandy and Joel's precis aloud and then discuss the reactive patterns you both observe in your marriage. List just two.

7. Using the two problem patterns, discuss and list an alternative way of relating under stress.

New	Response

8. 'Men are not often well prepared culturally for the task of sharing close thoughts and feelings with their wife.' Share with each other the ways you see this statement either validated or invalidated in your experiences.
The husband may be able to talk about his 'emotional education' in order to give insight into his functioning.

9. Schedule in a *non-doing* time to be together this coming week and share your answers to *Personal inventory* question 5.

✠ GROUP WORK

10. What, if any, would be the perceived problems couples would have if they knew everything about each other?

11. Under the *Barriers to intimacy* heading we state that we encounter people with a thousand ways of running from intimacy. Discuss among the group the ways you observe people avoiding intimacy.

12. Share the more successful ways you have found to grow closer to your spouse.

13. *'Storge'* is a really wonderful word. It pictures a secure feeling of belonging. Have the group share what their family unit does, or family of origin did, to express this sense of belonging.

14. Perhaps some are struggling with this concept and they need to experience *storge* now in the group. What can the group do to promote *storge* for each other?

6

Enjoy sexual love

'THE MAIN PROBLEM WITH SOME BOOKS about sexual love and marriage is that they don't really talk about sex frankly — the way it really is!' Alison had just shared some of the pain she felt and had asked about reliable books. Her plea touched both of us deeply.

She had been married now for three years. In learning to adjust sexually, Alison explained how she and her husband both desired to share full sexual satisfaction. 'But we nearly always find it difficult. We love each other, yet we seem to see and feel things differently! Why is it like that?'

'We'll have to find that out,' I answered. 'There could be any number of factors involved. But one thing I do know is that it's worth aiming at making it enjoyable and fulfilling for both of you.'

'My mother always told me sex was more for the man's pleasure than for mine,' said Alison. Already, we were starting to discover one of the blockages. I pointed out that one of the major problems facing young couples today is not just that good books on sex are often not known or read, but that there is a large amount of misinformation around — and believed!

Alison and John's story is all too common. In most Western countries, books on marriage and sex abound. But few of them are able to integrate beliefs and values

96

with this important dimension of the marital relationship. We want not only to answer the needs of couples to know the truth about sexual love and genuine fulfilment in their marriage, but for them to experience this. And as part of that, we want to assert the importance of integrating accurate knowledge on the one hand and values and attitudes that build safety and intimacy into our sexual relating on the other. To omit either is to short-change ourselves in sexual fulfilment in marriage.

What, then, are some of the essentials in sexual understanding for building a strong and fulfilling marriage? What makes great lovers? How differently do men and women see sex and love? What are the important attitudes and values that we need to bring to this area of our relationship?

These are just some of the issues addressed in this chapter.

✠ How does sexual love grow?

Sexual love grows from foundations of *trust, safety, respect, mutual acceptance* and *effective communication*. When any of these is lacking in a marriage, mutually satisfying sex is difficult.

Let's look at them one at a time.

❑ *Sexual love grows from trust*

When we begin to know and love someone, we begin to trust them. Before marriage, as trust increases, we share more of ourselves and, in turn, we enjoy the sense of being trusted. What we each begin to experience is shared trust, not only about the love we have for each other, but also about many other things. Special knowledge and trust means a growing intimacy at many levels — social, cognitive, emotional and spiritual.

In our clinics, we have seen hundreds of couples

seeking help with their marriages. Not uncommonly, trust is a major area of concern. It has never really grown, or it has been damaged by significant experiences.

It would be remiss of us not to comment on the fact that often the earliest damage to trust seems to have occurred, *usually for the female*, because the couple became heavily sexually involved prior to the commitment of marriage. We are not aware of any research evidence that indicates that heavy sexual involvement prior to marriage is helpful, despite the barrage of reassurance from the popular media. On the other hand, we *are* struck by the accumulation of clinical evidence suggesting that it actually damages trust and therefore leaves couples with a hurdle to get over in the ongoing development of deeper intimacy.

It seems to us that often full sexual involvement prior to the commitment of marriage crosses an initial boundary of trust that can leave each person unsure of the trustworthiness of his or her partner. It can also, of course, leave doubts about our own personal trustworthiness — and this is often accompanied by feelings of guilt. It seems to us that the setting and observing of appropriate limits to pre-marriage sexual intimacy provides a more solid basis for trust, safety and respect within the ongoing marriage.

Of course, there are many factors that can erode trust or prevent its normal growth in a marriage. Violent expressions of anger, an absence of time spent doing enjoyable things, manipulation, emotional withdrawal, infidelity, constant criticism or speaking disrespectfully — any of these and a host of other factors can impede the growth of trust between two people.

□ *Sexual love grows from a sense of safety*
Trust is the foundation underlying safety. If we don't trust our partner, we will not feel safe with him or her.

And because our sexual relating is affected by our fears and insecurities, we need to feel physically and emotionally safe if we are going to be able to relax and enjoy our sexuality with our spouse.

Somehow, we have to build a broad foundation of safety into our relationship. Without this, we will be inhibited and hesitant. Frequently, we will choose to avoid sexual relating, even though our desire is strong, because we fear ridicule, rejection or hurt.

❏ *Sexual love grows from a sense of respect*

As well as working to develop a deep level of trust and safety with each other, we need to be committed to an attitude of respect for one another. In the context of our sexuality, we need to learn how to show all the care, warmth and responsiveness of which we are capable, while still maintaining our sexual integrity and the respect due to each other.

Learning to express respect for one another in the area of our sexual relating involves avoiding the temptation to make our sexual relationship a battleground. It means avoiding the trap of punishing our spouse by withholding sex when we are angry or upset about something. Respect involves learning about each other's sexuality, each other's needs and being sensitive and caring in the way we handle this information.

❏ *Sexual love grows from effective communication*

Philip and Natalia were feeling uncomfortable. They were deep in discussion while we listened. 'When we cuddle, I feel you always want me to do more than that. Why can't we always stick to what we agreed?' she asked gently. 'This is one of the things that seems to cause a lot of our fights.'

'The problem for me,' said Philip, 'is that I seem to get aroused easily. Lots of times I know I'm imposing on Natalia, but I just feel the need so strongly that I pressure her into making love. I know it's not right and I often feel pretty lousy afterwards, but at the time it's pretty hard to stop.' He turned to me. 'Can you suggest how we can sort this out?'

Our response was the usual way we encourage couples in this area. 'Communicate with each other about your maleness and femaleness. In other words, talk about your sexual feelings and fears. Some people never break through to the point where they can talk about sex, so when they have struggles or problems, they can never address them. They're always guessing about what their partner thinks or feels. If you learn to talk about your sexual feelings, it will be a great help to you in handling them and it will give you a great freedom in your sexual relationship. So it's important to begin now learning to communicate clearly about your sexuality.'

Frequently, couples simply have not developed the freedom to talk about their sexual feelings and function with each other. Often this is because insufficient effort has gone into building trust and safety and respect.

If we are going to communicate effectively, we must develop a vocabulary that we are comfortable with to refer to body parts and the various aspects of lovemaking. We must take the risk of talking with each other, giving feedback on what feels nice and what is irritating, what helps us to relax and enjoy ourselves and what blocks enjoyment. We *must* talk to each other because we will never figure it out by guessing!

And we must also handle our partner's attempts to talk about his or her experience and feelings. There is so much riding on this! Many a couple has never learned to talk about their lovemaking because, at the first attempt, one or the other ridiculed something that was said. Be gracious here; be gentle and sensitive with one another. But, above all, start communicating!

❏ *Sexual love grows with mutual acceptance*
Mutual acceptance is another foundation for fulfilment in sexual love.

When Jenny and Tim came for help, they were both devastated. Up until recently, their love life had been great. But Tim had just returned from an overseas trip. He had missed Jenny more than usual this time and he had also missed his two boys. When he learned, within a few weeks of his return, that Jenny had developed a genital rash, his guilty conscience began to work.

She challenged him and Tim soon confessed his failures. These not only included unfaithfulness overseas and on earlier occasions, but lies told to cover up detection. Broken because of his failings, Tim was tearful and remorseful. Understandably, Jenny was deeply hurt and very angry. 'I feel so betrayed. My trust is shattered. Why did you deceive me for so long?' The question seemed to hang there endlessly. Tim had no answer.

With encouragement, Jenny was able to talk through her thoughts and feelings arising out of these painful revelations. Tim listened carefully and seemed ashamed. No excuses or defensive answers were offered. Deep repentance, asking for forgiveness and genuine graciousness from Jenny, eventually paved the way for restoration of the relationship. But it took months of counselling before trust, safety and respect began to grow again.

Healing of this kind always takes time. And always, new foundations must be laid.

Even now, though the sexual relationship has been restored, there is the occasional reminder of the past when Jenny's rash reappears. Continuing forgiveness is the only key to the healing of this incident. For this couple, to regain trust and respect enough to resume and enjoy their sexual love has been painful and costly.

Failure for Tim and Jenny required the development of a new mutual acceptance of each other. For Jenny, this meant being prepared not to raise issues from the past and not to entertain doubts, but to live in the forgiveness she was choosing to express. For Tim, it meant accepting little things in Jenny's personality or attitudes he had not previously liked. For both, there is now a new active love which accepts and values rather than criticises.

Mutual acceptance is critical in the area of sexuality, because there are many differences between men and women in this dimension. We detail these differences a little later on in this chapter. However, if these 'normal' differences are not understood and not accepted, then lovemaking is destined to be fraught with dangers rather than an experience of pleasure.

✠ What makes great lovers?

In our clinic, sexual therapy is a frequent adjunct to marriage counselling. One of the most common problems dealt with is lack of mutual sexual satisfaction. By definition, marriage requires each partner to satisfy the other over a lifetime. That is what makes great lovers! It is true mutual satisfaction, which implies total commitment by each to meeting the other's emotional and physical needs.

The problem often is that most men and women have very different standards for loving. Their basic ideas, expectations and values are different. Where sex should bring couples closeness and warmth, for many the sex act is lonely.

An American magazine with a circulation of seventy million had 90 000 responses to Ann Landers' question:

'Would you be content to be held close and treated tenderly and forget about "the act"?' More than seventy-one per cent, or 64 000 female respondents, said they preferred a warm hug or gentle touch to intercourse. It is worth noting that, of all the women who responded, forty per cent were *under* forty years of age!

The point here is that, overwhelmingly for women, the sex act without tenderness and emotional warmth is not satisfying. Sex in marriage is not an option, but neither is the caring and tender environment which needs to surround and permeate lovemaking.

Close friendship is another aspect of being great lovers. It is often not mentioned in this context and yet, without the mutuality of warmth and understanding generated by such close friendship in marriage, loving is not maximised. It is also this intimacy in friendship, the emotional sharing and relational warmth that flows from it, that sets the stage for enthusiastic physical oneness! If close friendship and all it implies is the thermometer to gauge the warmth of a marriage, then mutually satisfying sex is the pressure-gauge to measure the height and depth of the marriage relationship. Both measures are needed.

One woman we counselled complained to her husband: 'I feel sometimes I hardly know you at all. We are friendly, but we are not friends. You are just so private about your feelings and beliefs.' What she realised intuitively, yet without apparently experiencing it fully, was that emotional and spiritual warmth and depth are also linked intrinsically to physical love. In the discussion which followed, we were able to explain how feeling close through sharing the deeper parts of ourselves can often lead to a deepening of the physical union between a man and wife.

The same woman felt deprived sexually. 'If only you came to bed earlier, it might be different. We hardly ever have any time for quality communication, or sharing plans, let alone making love. I'm happy for you to exercise, but you spend at least two hours most nights working out at the gym, then you're too worn out to make love.' It turned out that this thirty-two year old husband was content with sexual intercourse not more than three or four times each month. His thirty-five year old wife, however, made it clear that she desired lovemaking at least twice a week. How can such differences be reconciled?

There is no simple or easy road. To be the great lovers we would like to be involves becoming whole people. It involves developing all aspects of our relationship. It involves learning to understand each other's needs and desires. For some, special healing from traumatic experiences may be required. For most, there will at least be a journey of changing wrong expectations of each other and learning to be more sensitive and caring in all our attitudes. And for all, it means willingness to detach ourselves from inappropriate influences and ideas. There will be concepts we have picked up (often along with things that are fine and good, or not-so-bad) in our families and from our peers.

We all need to work at enriching our marriages. Stimulating the friendship which is at the base of marriage is, as we have seen, essential.

But friendship alone is not enough. Maurice and Margaret discovered that. Their friendship began when they shared leadership of the senior high fellowship group of their church. It was always assumed their close friendship might lead on to marriage. Margaret had obviously been expecting an offer of marriage for some time.

Now, almost two years later, Maurice had still not proposed. He was puzzled himself by his lack of feelings. 'I don't seem to feel any warmth. Frankly, I've never been turned on romantically or sexually by her. We can talk about all sorts of things, but she seems more like a sister than anything.'

In counselling, Maurice came to see that the relationship was more limited than he thought. It contained lots of rational, intellectual sharing, but some spiritual elements and most of the emotional dimension was missing. Unless the relationship was ignited soon by the warmth of caring love, it would very likely fade right away. If taken onto marriage as it was, it would most certainly turn out to be dull, boring and completely unfulfilling for both. Here was the friendship, but without the fire of love.

There are some relationships which move onto marriage, where the friendship of love, even without sex, *has* been enough to sustain the marriage. These situations are difficult and always need special insight to help, if sexual love is to be kindled.

When Sarah and Doug first sought help, they had been married more than seven years. Before marriage, they had been friends for years. After marriage, the friendship remained strong, but sex was always difficult. It wasn't that love was absent; it was just that Sarah found it impossible to give or receive love. There were several complicating factors. Foremost was the abject refusal by Sarah's parents to show her affection as a child or to affirm her in any way. She hated her mother and could not remember being cuddled or ever sitting on either parents' knees.

Sarah's younger brother had received loving attention within the family. In counselling, Sarah recalled the anger, jealousy and disappointment she had felt at their different treatment, as early as six years of age.

'I knew I wasn't much good and I knew they didn't love me. But I still wanted their affection — to be loved. The trouble was they gave it all to him! I then decided I didn't need it, anyway. If you need affection, you must be weak. I've always hated being shown affection!'

The discovery of one of the roots of Sarah's' sexual problems was just as important as the earlier revelation of her having been sexually abused by a teacher, also in her early years. It was really not surprising that this couple needed sexual therapy. This is now ongoing.

What was surprising, however, was to find the great patience and loving understanding of this young husband. Doug's graciousness has somehow been sufficient for their friendship to sustain love, even without any full sexual expression, during the period of counselling.

Earlier counselling had not changed anything. If anything, it had made them more aware that the present situation without sex, let alone mutually satisfying sexual sharing, was intolerable. Now, with at least a willingness to tackle the roots of the problem, there is hope of Sarah being healed from her deprived past.

If she can be helped to wholeness, then this couple may become lovers at last. It is the fullness and wholeness of mutual sexual expression in marriage that each of us longs for.

✠ How is sexual lovemaking different for men and women?

Probably there is nothing which will help couples more to sexual fulfilment and oneness than husbands' understanding and acceptance of the differences in sexual functioning of their wives, and wives' similar understanding and acceptance of their husbands' differences. These differences between male and female functioning are many; and they are extremely important. Generally, they relate to differences, not only in orientation and perspective, but also in expectations, needs and responses concerning sex.

How often in counselling we have heard a wife say something like this: 'Sexually, he's an animal! He never seems to care or know how I'm feeling.' Or another says: 'His need always seems so urgent and so much greater than mine. He always wants sex!'

We also hear husbands say something like: 'She's frigid! She never seems to be interested in sex! Or: 'Occasionally, my wife seems to enjoy sex, but it's pretty rare — and only if I talk to her for a long time first.'

What, then, are some of these differences?

☐ *First, men and women are aroused differently*

With men, arousal is rapid and is usually stimulated visually or by imagining something sexual. The process is a very simple neurological reflex. With women, the process is usually much slower and, neurologically, more complex, with stimulation usually coming from expressions of tenderness and from the overall quality of the relationship.

This is why men can be sexually aroused when they see their wife undressing for bed, even though they may have had a fight over dinner and not spoken a word since. The wife, on the other hand, will probably feel completely repelled by the thought of making love. She feels no closeness; she does not feel valued or precious to her husband. There is no quality to the present relationship, nothing here to arouse her sexual desire at all.

☐ *Second, the man's orgasm is short and intense, while the woman's is longer and more in-depth*

This greater intensity is indicated by the fact that it is usually more difficult to distract the man, while the woman may be easily distracted. 'Are the kids all asleep?

Is the door closed? What's that noise?' Everything must be 'just right'.

Studies have shown that the average time taken by a male to achieve orgasm is between two and three minutes. The average time for a female is around thirteen minutes.

This is one of the reasons why it is so important for time to be spent in foreplay, so that the pleasure of achieving a climax can be shared by both husband and wife. Not infrequently, the cause behind a wife's lack of sexual interest lies in the fact that lovemaking is too rushed and her desire does not have a chance to develop. 'Bam. Slam. Thankyou, Ma'am' is not a good recipe for enjoyment by the wife!

☐ *Third, there are often differences in the number of orgasms that can take place at a time*

Often the woman is capable of more than one orgasm, or may sometimes be satisfied even without orgasm. The man is unable to have more than one orgasm without at least some recovery time in between and will rarely be satisfied without reaching his climax.

☐ *Fourth, the strength of the male sexual drive, at least as measured by desire for sex, is much greater than the female drive*

Of course, there are some marriages where, for varied reasons, the wife's physical desire for sex is greater than is the husband's. Whatever the case, it requires learning to adjust to the differing strengths of sexual desire.

We have no successful way of quantifying the different strengths of male and female sexual desire but, if we could, it would not surprise us to find that while both male and female sexual drives are strong, the usual quantitative strength of the male desire is several times, perhaps even many times, greater than that of the female.

Multimillion dollar industries in pornography and prostitution run almost exclusively on the strength of the male sex drive. Thus, when wives accuse their husbands of 'always wanting sex' and husbands accuse their wives of 'being frigid', it may well turn out that they are actually accusing their partner of normality! They are simply making the mistake of judging their partner's sexuality through the filter of what is 'normal' for them.

In general, men roll off the assembly line desiring sex more frequently than women. When these differences are not understood and accepted, and loving adjustments made between husband and wife, then it is not uncommon for a lot of blaming and conflict to develop.

☐ Fifth, men and women differ in the significance placed on sex

While the survey by Ann Landers noted above indicates that, for a majority of women, intercourse is not necessarily the most important expression of love, for most men it assuredly is. While intercourse for men is obviously an action centred around a physical release, it is completely reductionistic to think that that is all it is. Most men will tell you that it is also the action, above all others, in which they feel most close to their wife — the best expression of their in-loveness, their intimacy.

Given that this is what it means to males, it is not surprising that often they feel so totally crushed when they are accused of just 'using me'. The point is not to plead for a new understanding of the purity of men's motives in lovemaking — there certainly is a selfish component — but there is also, usually, a component which best expresses for them their feelings of being close, of being in love.

Understanding these basic differences are crucial for the couple who desire fulfilment in their lovemaking. Because

the husband loves his wife, he will recognise the importance of constantly valuing her and affirming her, so that
the relationship is secure and intimate. Out of his love for
her, he will seek to restrain his sexual demands at times.
Out of love for her, he will seek to develop his capacity
to hug and cuddle, without putting any additional sexual
pressure on her.

For her part, out of her love for her husband, the wife
will seek to meet his sexual needs more often than she
personally needs. In a context of loving and valuing each
other, the journey of sexual compatibility and fulfilment
will be successful over time. It should never be anticipated
that it will be instantly successful.

If husbands will give priority to helping their wife feel
loved and cherished, not just desired for sexual fulfilment
and treated shabbily the rest of the time, another major
blockage will have been addressed.

'So often I just feel less than a person. I feel used!'
This was Judy's response in a recent counselling session
when I asked how she felt about her lovemaking with her
husband.

Jim exploded. 'I don't know what I'm expected to do!
When we first got married, Judy said I was good. I could
make it last for up to ten minutes. Now after three kids
and twelve years on, she doesn't seem nearly so interested.
I'd be happy if Judy could enjoy sex just two or three
times a *month*, but now it's usually just a case of "Hurry
up and get it over with." What's a guy supposed to do?'

This was an untenable situation. Both were lonely;
neither felt satisfied. There seemed to be no sense of
acceptance of the other or sacrificial love. It took several
sessions of counselling before Jim began to learn the basic
lesson about communication of the total person.

Judy's response was also slow. She had been so
damaged by lack of response that it took quite a while for

romantic love to be rekindled. As Jim learned to share more openly about himself and to be less self-focussed, to want to please Judy in their times together, he somehow seemed to change before her very eyes.

She began to view him differently and began to enjoy him as well as herself in their lovemaking. In their case, although it was a slow process, love was literally reborn! Affection and intimacy became intrinsic to their relationship, while quality in their sexual encounters replaced the pressures they had felt previously.

These changes are possible for every couple, no matter how unfulfilling or difficult their lovelife has become. But they will require action — change. Words on paper will achieve nothing and counselling will be a waste of time unless changes are made. Nothing can save us from this hard piece of reality.

✠ How important is fidelity?

Fidelity is the *sine qua non* of sexual fulfilment. This Latin phrase means, literally, 'without which, nothing'. If we don't build our sexual relationship on a platform of fidelity, we will be hugely short-changed in sexual fulfilment.

How many couples, or individuals, have set out to disprove the statement above? They have been 'liberated'. They are adult enough to handle and enjoy the excitement of wife-swapping, or a fling here and there. How many marriages, their wreckage strewn across the landscape of society, does it take before we acknowledge that it doesn't work? Infidelity is, commonly, *lethal*. Full stop.

Of course, we don't want it to be so. We want to believe that cheating is okay, that it 'needn't necessarily' be damaging to my marriage if I have an affair. Sure. The trouble is, all the reassurances in the world don't seem to settle our emotions down when we discover that we've been cheated on!

It's not hard to figure out why. Human sexuality is such an area of vulnerability, an area with so many of our insecurities about self-worth attached, that we simply cannot cope with the shadow of another person hanging across this part of our life.

When we are sexually unfaithful, we trade off the unique fulfilment of deep intimacy for the momentary excitement of sexual variety. There are plenty who will try to persuade us that it's a good trade-off. Something programmed deep within our spirit tells us it isn't.

✠ Should we keep quiet about sex?

There is an unhealthy attitude to sexuality peddled by some that would suggest that this is an area of our functioning that should not be talked about. This attitude conveys the sense that there is something dirty or distasteful about human sexuality and that the less we acknowledge, or express, our sexuality, the more noble we will be. Nothing could be further from the truth.

We are sexual beings. We should celebrate our sexuality unashamedly, giving energy to learning how to integrate this part of who we are with the other important parts of our being. It goes wrong when we try to deny our sexuality altogether; and it goes wrong when we treat it as though it is everything, or the most important part. It is good to enjoy, to take pleasure in each other's physical body. It is good to enjoy gazing upon each other in the context of lovemaking and to exult in the feelings of sexual pleasure that we can give and receive. This is a great gift, not to be lightly discarded.

A fulfilling sexual relationship should certainly not be the only goal in marriage. If it is, it will never be achieved. But, in its proper place, it will be one of the key building blocks for the marriage that is moving onto a deep maturity.

Questions for thought and discussion

✠ PERSONAL INVENTORY

In chapter 6, the importance of sexual love in marriage is emphasised. Understanding more about our sexual differences and responses also helps in making better lovers. Achieving sexual satisfaction in the context of marriage commitment is based on a deepening sensitivity to each other as well as emotional intimacy and friendship.

Mutual understanding of each other's needs, both sexual and emotional, with ability to communicate in these areas, will enable us to strengthen our marriage. Also, understanding the basis of our human sexuality — how we are made, male and female differences — will encourage us to wholeness in our marriage.

If our sexual love is to be fully satisfying, it will need to be seen in perspective. Integrating the physical, emotional, thinking and spiritual aspects of our relationship is important.

How can we best achieve this? Obviously, it won't just happen by wanting. We have found that couples who are prepared to work at knowing and understanding more, who can talk to each other openly about all these aspects of their relationship, do best. So, take your time now individually, as well as together, to reflect on your responses to the following questions.

1. Do you recall whether or not, in your adolescence or later, it was your parents or others who prepared you by talking about sex and marriage? How was it done?

2. From your present perspective, in what areas and aspects of sexuality and marriage would you have liked your parents or others to have shared more deeply?

3. What has been the easiest aspect of your sexual relationship?

4. What has been the most difficult?

5. How easy is it for you to talk about sexual issues with your spouse? Why?

6. Is trust easy, not so easy, or difficult with your spouse? Is it important? Why?

7. How important is sharing emotionally for you and your spouse? Does this make an impact on your sexual love?

8. How important is it for you to share ideas or to discuss knowledge about things or other people with your spouse? Does this in any way make a difference to your sexual love?

9. Do you and your spouse share or discuss spiritual concepts or ideas, or pray together? What difference, if any, does this make in your sexual love?

10. How satisfied are you with the amount of affection you receive from your spouse?

11. Are you sometimes/often reluctant to be affectionate with your spouse because it is interpreted as a sexual advance? How do you think you can change this?

12. How do you think you can improve the ways of ensuring your sexual relationship is enjoyable, interesting and satisfying?

13. Are you and your spouse agreed fully about your decisions on birth control and family planning? What fears do you still have?

14. How important to you is:
    a. touching?
    b. kissing?
    c. being physically close?
    d. being emotionally and spiritually close?
    Why?

15. When do you feel most loved?
    When do you feel most sexually fulfilled?

16. Do you ever use sex with, or refuse sex to, your spouse unfairly?
    Will you change this or resolve to discuss it soon?

✠ SHARING WITH YOUR PARTNER

After you have personally considered and responded to the above questions, use them as a stimulus for joint discussion. Set time aside as a priority to communicate about your sexual relationship with your spouse to make sure your lovemaking is enjoyable and fulfilling. By integrating your sexuality with all other parts of your lives, you will gain perspective and satisfaction so that your marriage will be strengthened.

✠ GROUP WORK

17. Discuss the effect of your different experiences of parental guidance in sexual matters and their relationship to marriage.

18. How effective was your experience of preparation for marriage, especially in understanding sexual love?

19. Which of the male/female differences is most helpful to your understanding of your sexual relationship? Share in the group.

20. What common problems arise because of male/female sexuality differences? How can these best be overcome?

21. What are the most common fears associated with our sexual functioning? What would be most helpful in overcoming these? Discuss.

Part C:
Maintenance

7

Speak your love

IN MANY PARTS OF WESTERN SOCIETY, it has become almost a cultural norm to ridicule your spouse. Comedians ridicule their partners as they do their routines, often getting big laughs as they disparage things such as a spouse's looks, intelligence and sexual appetite, right down to things like her (or his) cooking and driving. It's all one big hearty laugh — or so we tell ourselves.

Television shows follow or perhaps even lead! Think of some of the pathetic shows that have been foisted on us over recent years as sitcoms about marriage and/or family life. Many of them rely heavily on put-down humour directed at the spouse to produce their laughs. Sadly, we often laugh without realising the modelling effect this manner of speaking has. And all too easily we reproduce it in our own marriage.

At parties, all too frequently, husbands and wives join in the conversation by telling everyone else some tale that displays their spouse's inadequacy or folly. 'That's nothing,' Jane will say. 'Tony's away so much for work that he has to relearn the children's names every time he comes back home.' Everyone laughs accordingly in response to this little humorous gem.

On another occasion, Tony will get a laugh from everyone with his story about Jane's sense of direction — so hopeless that the other day she drove out of a service station back the way she had come, without even realising it!

It's all done for fun — no hurt intended. At least, that's the defence people use as they drive home in the car afterwards, when they are confronted with a hurt, angry spouse. Many of the best fights between husband and wife occur after a party as one confronts the other with the dreaded question: 'Why did you say that?' The truth is, 'spouse assassination' contains disguised anger — and it is always destructive to relationship.

It has even become fashionable with some to have a disparaging nickname for a spouse — 'the Ayatollah', 'little Hitler', or 'the dragon'! Again, it usually gets passed off as humour, but it never seems very funny to the person on the receiving end. Instead, hurts accumulate and walls go up — and people wonder why there doesn't seem to be much closeness in their marriage relationship.

'Sticks and stones will break my bones, but names will never hurt me.' The saying sounds wise, but most of us do not live long before we discover that, in fact, words can be very hurtful. We can be deeply wounded by the things that are said to us and about us.

It is no accident that the Bible instructs us to be careful about how we use our tongue. There, one of the writers, who doesn't seem inclined to beat around the bush, describes our tongues as ' a fire. . . a world of evil among the parts of the body'.

The point clearly is that our tongues have a huge amount of destructive potential. Used as a weapon against a spouse, our tongues can destroy love rapidly and effectively. Our tongues have the power of life and death for our marriage.

Our clinical experience validates this warning. So often, the words that have been spoken in a moment of raw anger have wounded a husband or wife so deeply that they struggle to forgive. Many marriages have been destroyed primarily because one or both partners never learned to tame their tongue. Their tongue became a piercing sword, an instrument of death to their marriage.

Yet it need not be this way. The same tongue that can be an instrument of death in a marriage can be an instrument of life! It is vital that we seek to develop a consistency between our claim to love our spouse and the way we speak to, and about, him or her.

If we are to take seriously the call to love one another in our speech, there is simply no room for developing habits of 'knocking', 'bagging' or 'putting down' our spouse in the way we speak. We put our marriage at risk to the extent that we ignore this truth.

✠ Important findings from Mehrebian's research

One source of information about the impact of our communication upon others is a classic piece of research done by Mehrebian in 1971. He was interested in assessing the impact of some of the components of communication upon the receiver. Amongst other things, he found that whether the receiver liked the person speaking, or disliked them, was a function of variables such as: the *content* of the message (i.e. the words actually spoken), the *tone* of the person's voice and the *facial expression* associated with the communication.

One of Mehrebian's most significant findings was that: *total liking = 7% verbal liking + 38% vocal liking + 55% facial liking*. In this statement he is equating 'verbal' with the words spoken, 'vocal' with voice tone and 'facial' with the sender's facial expression.

Think of it for a moment. The actual words we speak have only a seven per cent impact for liking or disliking upon the hearer! Our voice tone contributes thirty-eight per cent — and our facial expression contributes a huge fifty-five per cent of the impact! Amongst other things, this means that we read non-verbal cues as much stronger and truer than verbal messages when we are receiving a communication.

What are the implications of Mehrebian's findings?

First, words alone are not enough
Clearly, these findings demonstrate that it's not enough to throw the words 'I love you' at our spouse every now and then and assume that this fulfils the need to speak lovingly.

While we would never want to under-emphasise the importance of telling a spouse that we love him or her, the significance of the words will be largely determined by *how* we say them — by our voice, tone and the accompanying facial expression. The words alone may have only a seven per cent impact — and this will be hugely outweighed by other messages if our voice tone is really saying: 'Give me a break, will you? Why do you always have to be pestering me by asking if I love you? Can't you see I'm busy reading this book?'

For our spouse to receive a strong affirmation of our love, we will need to speak in such a way that our voice tone and our non-verbal communication also says, 'I love you.'

Second, the medium is the message
As well as the warning above, however, there is a very encouraging aspect to Mehrebian's findings. His research suggests that, almost regardless of the content, I can be giving messages of affirmation and love to my spouse if the *way* I speak, the medium, conveys these qualities. The

truth is that I can be talking with my wife about a blocked kitchen drain (content only has seven per cent impact), and yet my voice tone and facial expression can be giving messages of respect and affirmation. If I'm doing it right, I can be communicating about a drain and yet giving a ninety-three per cent impact message of 'and I love you — you're precious to me.' I kind of like that!

This means that I have the freedom, no matter what the content of the communication, to be also communicating love and affirmation, providing my voice tone and facial expression are caring. Although I will want to tell my wife that I love her clearly and unequivocally at times, I can tell her this same message in virtually all my communication with her. Somehow, it's a liberating discovery! It means that it is even possible for me to disagree with my wife, yet to do it in a way that overwhelmingly affirms her as a person. The medium conveys a stronger message than the words.

Hence, in our clinics, we take time to teach people how to speak so that the voice tone and non-verbals are all communicating 'You are important to me, I value and respect you, I love you.' If we can get the person's way of speaking right, we will have done much to remove destruction and replace it with life.

✠ The skills we need to develop to speak our love

For many of us, the task of learning to speak our love will not come easily. We may have been exposed to models of power and control rather than of love in the communication patterns of our parents. We may have heard our father order our mother around, or our mother scream abuse and hatred at our father, as we grew up.

We may have learned to use our words and our

communication methods to exert power over others or to protect ourselves.

Learning to communicate with our spouse in ways that bring us closer together may be, at one and the same time, both exciting and scary. If this sounds like you, be assured that you are not alone in feeling this ambivalence. But the journey is still immensely worthwhile. Your heart already confirms this.

What are the specific ingredients that we need to work on if we are to learn to speak our love?

First, we need to listen
Have you ever had the experience of having someone listen and express caring for you at a time when you were struggling with some aspect of life? How different that response is to the person who brushes off your feelings or your struggle with a 'pat answer', or who whacks you over the head with a quick-fix piece of advice. How often do we 'wage help' at hurting people instead of listening and caring.

When someone listens to us, they give us a precious gift. Their time and active attention affirms us as people and affirms the importance of what troubles or concerns us. Even if they don't have one constructive suggestion, we often feel helped because they care. Listening communicates love.

Clinical practice has shown us that men in our society are often particularly poor listeners. Frequently, husbands show a very limited capacity to listen caringly. They tend to want to rush in and give six suggestions for how to 'fix' things and then move onto something else. Often, the reason is that in their work they are paid to make decisions, to solve problems. They have trouble realising that a marriage requires different skills to their occupation. Tending a garden is different to running a rail service!

They don't easily see why their wife is not appreciative of their good advice — why, in fact, she gets angry at them when all they have done is try to help.

What they need to realise is that if this is occurring, it is probably true that they are giving advice, when what their wife wants is for them to listen. . . and care. Sometimes, advice *is* cheap and the recipient feels unvalued. A simple way to overcome the problems generated in this kind of situation is for the question to be asked: 'What do you want me to do? Do you want me to offer advice, or do you want me to just listen and let you talk out your feelings?'

Asking this question will head off a lot of misunderstandings. If the answer is 'I want you to listen', then the task becomes one of giving active attention, not intruding too much, avoiding giving advice or trying to 'fix' things — in other words, listening and caring. The skill of becoming a better listener simply requires a willingness — and practice!

It is not a passive role. There is certainly room for questions to clarify what the person is sharing. And some personal responses will always be important, too. A response such as, 'Wow, that was unfair,' shows that you are listening and that you are supportive.

But don't intrude too much. Let your eyes, your face and your body posture indicate your care. A touch on the arm or taking your partner's hand will probably speak more eloquently than a mouthful of words.

Second, we need to share our feelings
One of the most important ways that we speak our love is by working at sharing our feelings. Again, this is a skill that will not always come easily.

If one or other of you has come from a dysfunctional family, it well may be a huge task. In dysfunctional families, we often learn the lesson: 'Don't share how you feel. People can't cope with your feelings. Feelings are to be ignored.'

The truth is quite different to the lessons from such a family. The truth is that sharing our feelings with our spouse and with others brings us closer to them — it deepens our level of intimacy. Certainly, at times we may feel helpless. We may not know how to respond to the tears, the frustration or the anger — or even the full-on joy — being expressed by our spouse. Probably, at times like this, the best thing we can do is remind ourselves that our task is not to 'fix' (who can 'fix' the tears of a partner who is grieving?). Our task is just to listen and care and, if we can do that well, we will have been helpful.

Now, of course, how our feelings are treated when we share them is crucial in all of this. People can easily mistreat the feelings shared by their marriage partner. Feelings need primarily to be *accepted*. Things go wrong when someone says to us, 'You shouldn't feel like that.' For the most part, we don't have a lot of control over our feelings.

So if our feelings are *not* accepted — if instead they are 'corrected' or rejected — we will usually learn not to share them again. Having someone tell us we shouldn't feel a certain way is about as useful as someone telling us when we are weeping, 'Don't be sad; be happy!' If only it were that easy.

So for each of us, the task is to listen and to accept the feelings shared by our partner, even when these feelings make us a bit anxious. Often as feelings are shared and accepted, some of the intensity goes from them and the speaker feels much more in control.

✠ Dialoguing, a technique for learning to speak your love

One of the most valuable techniques for learning to speak lovingly with our spouse is the technique that has been called 'dialoguing'. It has been outlined in one of the chapters of John Powell's book, *The Secret of Staying in Love*, and is used extensively in Marriage Encounter weekends and in Growing Together in Marriage programs. (These are excellent programs for married couples to attend as they instruct, model and give opportunity to develop comunication.)

The technique of dialoguing involves three parts. The first part is writing a ten-minute love letter to your spouse on a set topic. Your marriage partner does the same thing. The second part involves exchanging letters and reading what your spouse has written, usually two times through at least. In the third part, the two of you talk (dialogue) about what has been shared in the letters, usually for about ten minutes.

Let's look at each part separately for further clarification.

THE FIRST STEP: *the ten-minute love letter*

The most important thing about the letter is that it be written *as a love letter*. It is intended to be a loving communication. This emphasis will affect the whole tone of the letter.

The letter should start with a term of affection, such as 'My darling Stuart. . .', 'Dearest Ellen. . .' using some such term of endearment. It should also be signed off in a way appropriate to a love letter, with words such as 'with all my love. . .'

The body of the letter should be made up of your thoughts and feelings about the set topic, with a special emphasis on feelings. The truth is that when we share our feelings honestly with our spouse, we give them a precious gift for we share our deepest self.

The letter should be written in a free-flowing style, with no concern about spelling or punctuation. This is not an English examination! The only issue of concern in this area is: 'Can I understand what is written?' If so, finer details of the art of writing are irrelevant. This needs to be kept in mind so that no judgmental comments are made.

The letter-writing time should be limited to ten minutes. If the writer goes at it, without editing or trying to write a definitive life-statement, usually three-quarters of a page to a couple of pages of writing will result. Variations occur because some people write larger, some write faster, some are more compulsive (and so have to get it right!) and so on. The important thing is simply to put down your thoughts and feelings about the topic as a meaningful sharing of something of yourself. Don't think too hard — just write!

Letters may be written at the same pre-arranged time, such as before going to bed at night, or they may be written at different times during the day by the marriage partners.

THE SECOND STEP: *the exchange of the letters*
Letters are exchanged and read at a set time. Again, for many people the most convenient time may be towards the end of the day.

Letters should be received as a gift. The appropriate way to receive a gift is to say, 'Thankyou'.

Letters should be read through at least twice, before dialoguing begins. The second reading should be perhaps a little more leisurely, reading with your heart as well as your understanding. This part of the process will usually only take a few minutes.

THE THIRD STEP: *dialoguing*

The third part of the process is roughly limited to ten minutes also, although if the sharing is rich it may be extended by the couple.

The most important parts of the dialoguing process involve understanding the purpose of dialoguing and the communication techniques best suited to achieving this purpose. The purpose of dialoguing is to understand your partner. It is not intended to be a technique for judging, or changing, your partner! When it goes astray, these are usually the things that cause the problem.

Since understanding is the aim, what communication techniques are legitimate in this period of back-and-forth sharing? The first is asking questions for clarification. For example, if a person has written in his or her letter, 'When I was young, I felt loved by my parents' and no further information is given about this point, it would be entirely appropriate to ask questions like, 'What did you parents do to show you that you were loved?' or 'What did it do for you, knowing that you were loved and wanted?'

How, when, where, what and *why* questions are all useful in filling out the picture, so that you understand your spouse even better, although it's a good idea not to overdo the *why* questions.

A second legitimate communication technique to use in this sharing time is making a personal response. Here, instead of asking a question to further my understanding about something that has been written, I talk about how I felt when I read some part of the letter. For example, I might say: 'When I read this part where you said you felt loved by your parents, I thought, "Yeah, that shows up in you all the time. You're secure in knowing that you're okay." To be honest, I felt a little bit envious, too.'

This is a personal response which shares how I felt when I read part of your letter. It is particularly useful in promoting understanding between marriage partners. And the purpose of dialoguing is to help understand each other better!

Some responses are definitely ruled out. For example, it is not acceptable to ridicule or to try to change your partner's feelings. Responses like, 'That's ridiculous', 'You shouldn't think that' or 'This bit really doesn't make sense to me' are illegitimate. They are really subtle attempts to change your partner. Dialoguing is about understanding, not changing each other!

Obviously, from what we have emphasised earlier in this chapter, voice tone and non-verbal communication will be important in this sharing time. Voice tone should be gentle and loving, communicating tenderness and affection. Facial and body messages, including eye-contact, should be saying, 'You're precious to me.'

The actual process in this third part involves one person beginning by asking questions for further clarification on something that has been written in the letter he or she has just read and then allowing time for the partner to respond. Or it may begin by one person speaking of his or her personal response to some part of the letter.

It is usually good for one person to clarify and respond for a while before switching roles and focussing on the other person's letter. As you get more comfortable with the process, a relaxed flow back and forth begins to develop.

As stated already, the central and immediate purpose of dialoguing is to understand one another better by using a fairly safe, self-sharing technique of letter-writing and discussing. The longer-term purpose is to develop communication skills so that you can share comfortably and deeply with each other on topics of mutual concern, without the necessity of writing a letter to begin the process.

Although it is perfectly all right to set a topic for dialoguing that is relevant to your immediate situation, it

is often good to begin by writing and sharing on pre-s
topics. We offer some below just to get you going, but
you can quickly develop your own. Perhaps to begin
with you might aim to do three dialogues per week.
Choose topics that seem most relevant to your life situations. If you persist, you will quickly deepen your
understanding of each other and you will notice that your
skills and feeling of safety in communication grow rapidly.

Many of these topics have been adapted from John
Powell's book, *The Secret of Staying in Love*, or from
Marriage Encounter weekends.

1. What were the most important 'life-messages' you
   learned from your childhood? How did you learn
   them and how do you feel about them now?
2. How did your father live out the roles of being a
   husband and father? How do you feel about what
   he modelled and its effect on you?
3. How did your mother live out her roles of being a
   wife and mother? How do you feel about what
   she modelled and its effect on you?
4. If someone asked you, 'Who are you?', and you
   had to respond with two descriptive words, what
   would they be? Explain what you mean by each
   one and how you feel about them. You might
   also find it useful to try your hand at identifying
   two words that best describe your spouse. Explain
   what you mean by these words and how you feel
   about them.
5. What roles were you required to take in your
   family during your growing-up years? What
   effects has this had upon you and how do you
   feel about these effects?
6. If someone who loved you asked you, 'What can I do
   to show my love for you?', how would you respond?

7. If you had to face death in the near future, what would you like people to remember about you? How would you feel about your achievements and the way you have lived your life so far?

8. Share from your memories three experiences when you felt humiliated or crushed. Describe the incidents, especially how you felt at the time.

9. Share from your memories three experiences when you really felt affirmed and loved by others. Describe the incidents, especially the feelings you had at the time.

10. If you really trusted someone and they said, 'I love you', how would you feel inside? How do you feel about giving and receiving love?

11. How do I feel about our children and what are my hopes for their futures? Be specific about each one.

12. How do I feel about improvements in our marriage relationship and our communication?

13. What are the three most precious things in my life, not counting people or pets? Why are they so important to me?

14. What is one change that I have made in myself and how do I feel about it?

15. What books have had the biggest impact on me during my life? What did I get from them?

16. What are my reasons for wanting to go on living?

17. What are my reasons for wanting to go on living with you?

18. What are the qualities that most attracted me to you in our courting days?

19. I think I need your help in. . .

20. What are my feelings about our sexual relationship?

21. What qualities do I like best in you? How does this make me feel?

22. What qualities do I like best in myself? How does this make me feel?

23. What do I like best about us as a couple? How does this make me feel?

24. What are the ways I hide myself or protect myself from other people? How do I feel about these?

25. In what areas am I least willing to listen to you? How does my answer make me feel?

26. What feelings do I have that I find most difficult to share with you? Describe the feelings as fully and carefully as you can.

27. What is the atmosphere in our home like? How do I feel about this?

28. How can we better express our love for each other in public situations?

29. What are the things that I really enjoy? How do they make me feel?

30. What are my feelings when you say you need me?

31. How do I feel about myself today and how does this make me feel about you?

32. How do I feel when you listen to me caringly and attentively?

33. What are my feelings when I know I have hurt you?

34. How do I feel when I am too tired to give to our relationship?

35. How do I feel when I know that you are proud of me?

36. What movie or movies have had the biggest impact on my life? What did I get from them?

37. How do I feel when you have done something to make me happy?

38. What is the nicest thing you have done for me this week and how do I feel about it?

39. What do I think God is trying to teach me about at the moment? How do I feel about his promptings?

40. How do I feel about my relationship with your family?

Questions for thought and discussion

✠ PERSONAL INVENTORY

Many of the deepest wounds and most severe bullet-holes that individuals carry into life have come from the tongue of someone who was a significant person in their life.

Parents have told their children, 'You're nothing but a stupid idiot. You'll never amount to anything!' and the message has been received. The child's spirit has been deeply wounded and he or she struggles with self-doubt and feelings of inferiority throughout the rest of life or until healing is sought.

The same damage can so easily be done in a marriage

relationship. Many couples live with the legacy of hurtful words, poured out on each other in times of anger. They aren't sure that they are safe from further abuse or attack. And the result is that they never let themselves get too close. Intimacy is stifled; it's too risky.

The good news is that the opposite is also possible. Our tongues can be instruments of encouragement, reassurance and healing for others, including our spouse. And whatever has been in the past can be different and better from now on if we seek to change destructive patterns.

This is a time to get dead-set honest with yourself. Don't pretty yourself up if the truth isn't too pretty. Examine honestly the ways you have used your tongue, for good and for bad, in your marriage.

1. What model did I get from my mother and father about how to speak to a spouse? How has this affected me?

2. What destructive habits have I included in my speaking to my spouse over the years?
   - use of sarcasm
   - verbal abuse
   - screaming/shouting
   - name-calling
   - lying
   - controlling by guilt
   - other

3. If I have made use of any of the above, how has this affected my spouse — and the quality of our marriage?

4. What positive qualities have I built into the way I speak to my spouse?

5. Who do I respect because of the way they speak to and about their spouse? What are the positive qualities I can see in their manner of speaking?

6. What is one quality in my manner of speaking I could begin to work on eliminating right now (e.g. sarcasm, ridicule)?

7. What one quality in my manner of speaking could I begin to work on adding or increasing right now (e.g. speaking encouragingly)?

✠ SHARING WITH YOUR PARTNER

8. Share with each other your answers to questions 6 and 7 above and ask your partner to help you. Be aware that this is risk territory for each of you, so it is very important that you focus on encouraging and supporting positive change, not on pointing out failures. Pray for each other right now in regard to the changes you want to make.

9. Give honest, loving feedback to each other on how you see your partner's voice tone and non-verbal cues in your communication. This is a chance to benefit by learning how someone else sees these features of your communication and by working on changes that would be positive.

10. Ask each other for forgiveness now for the hurts that have accumulated over the years from your communication with each other. You may benefit by speaking specifically about one or two hurtful incidents, times or patterns, but be careful to make the focus one of understanding better, not of dumping blame or trying to induce guilt.

11. Practise speaking your love to each other right now, by taking time to let your spouse know three specific things about him or her that you appreciate and why these mean so much to you.

✠ GROUP WORK

12. Take time to share in the group an incident or time when someone said something, either positive or negative, to you that had an ongoing impact on your life and functioning.

13. Recall a time when you really sought to speak words of encouragement or help to someone. How did it go? Share with the group.

14. Take it in turns to speak a word of affirmation and encouragement to the person on your left as you go around the group. Discuss afterwards how you found this task and, also, how you felt when you were being affirmed.

15. Share in the group your plan for making *one* positive change in the way you speak to your spouse. Be as specific as you can.

8

Learn to handle the hassles

TERRY AND FIONA HAD BEEN MARRIED two years when they came seeking marriage counselling. Both deeply committed Christians, they were, nevertheless, fighting a lot and could see that their relationship was being damaged.

Terry's characteristic style of arguing was to explode with anger and the force of his explosion was often quite frightening for Fiona. He would scream and swear, calling her names that were deeply hurtful. His anger outbursts were so violent that he had physically attacked his wife on a few occasions, slapping her face and pushing her against a wall. Terry's father had handled his anger this way and Terry had not yet left this bit of junk from his family of origin behind.

For her part, Fiona handled anger by withdrawing into herself. This had been Fiona's pattern all her life. She had been raised in a home where the father had a problem with alcohol and she had learned there that anger was unacceptable, so she tended to deny her anger. However, she was capable of punishing even the slightest fault in Terry very effectively by her withdrawals and he suffered anguish during these periods. She would stop talking to him, would refuse to go anywhere with him and would not do things, such as the housework, with him.

While his style of expressing anger in conflict situations

was immensely damaging, hers was no less destructive to the marriage relationship. She had not yet learned to leave this bit of *her* past behind.

Time was rapidly running out for this marriage. Already, the hurts had accumulated and both reminded me of badly wounded soldiers as they shared their story in my office. It was clear that they could not take much more. It was also apparent that their whole approach to handling conflicts or disagreements was a disaster.

We had to work out a way of enabling them to move through a disagreement without wounding each other so much. I knew that I would have to give such a volatile couple a very clear structure to work from.

✠ How 'puffers' and 'stuffers' create hassles

People often come into marriage with major problems in their handling of disagreements and arguments. Essentially, they have not learned to handle their anger in any constructive way. Some explode. They have been called 'puffers'!

Others hold their anger in, sometimes not recognising that it still comes out, usually in passive-aggressive ways. They have been called 'stuffers'!

Any combination of these people has its problems. Two puffers in a marriage will produce a lot of damage unless they learn better ways of handling their anger. Two stuffers will gradually choke off love by punishing each other in hurtful withdrawal. A puffer and a stuffer together, as was the case with Terry and Fiona, will be equally destructive. The stuffer's approach will fuel the puffer's anger, while the puffer's violence will frighten or cause a total loss of respect over time for the stuffer.

Occasionally, a puffer will be so violent in his explosions that he will be what has been termed a 'rage-aholic'. Rage-aholics are people whose violence is so great that they are capable of immense verbal explosions, often accompanied by violence to people and property. Often their explosions are unpredictable. They are likely to physically and verbally thrash other family members for sustained periods over something as trivial as the toilet roll being put on 'the wrong way', or someone washing a dish 'the wrong way'. Rage-aholics terrify their partners and leave their children emotionally shattered.

Rage-aholics need <u>professional help</u> to change their pattern of handling anger. Otherwise, the trail of destruction they leave is immense. And their destructive pattern will almost certainly be passed onto some of their children, destroying the children's ability to find intimacy in marriage.

Many people are puffers and many are stuffers. Far too many are rage-aholics. Such people need simple, clear guidelines to enable them to work through the normal conflicts in marriage, without mortally wounding their marriage relationship.

✠ How mapping can help us handle hassles

Alan, a good friend of mine, was excited. He had come to lunch with me and we were catching up. Somehow, the topic of communication in marriage had arisen and Alan was sharing a method he and his wife, Jenny, had discovered that enabled them to really listen to each other and communicate at depth where each was at.

I listened with interest as he talked about *mapping*. Already I was thinking about a few couples that might benefit from this technique. But I was thinking that it could also be applied to their handling of conflict. It would provide a structure and force them to listen to each other. One such couple was Terry and Fiona.

Tony Buzan, author of several books in the area of brain functioning and creative learning methods, developed the concept in the 1970s of mindmapping as a tool for enhancing people's note-taking. In more recent years, mindmapping has been developed as a technique for enhancing learning in many different situations. Perhaps its primary value for us in our area of interest lies in the fact that it provides a system for organising ideas around an area of conflict.

The specific technique suggested by Alan has built on Buzan's mindmapping system, but also incorporated some differences that Alan and Jenny had found valuable. Here are the steps for you to follow:

Step 1: Each of you needs to take equal responsibility to monitor your communication so that you recognise the beginning of a conflict or argument.
Each of you needs to have equal responsibility to stop before the hostilities escalate. This is usually done by one of you simply saying something like: 'Hey, we're in conflict over this. Let's stop the arguing and work it through using mapping skills.' If emotions are running very high, it may be advisable to postpone this for a little while to allow yourselves to cool down a bit.

Step 2: Grab a sheet of paper and a pen. Draw a circle in the middle of the page. Write the issue in the centre of the circle. For example, if the subject is 'finances', write that in the circle.

Step 3: One of you begins sharing while the other writes. The listener (writer) draws a line out from the circle like the spoke of a wheel and tries to summarise the essence of the speaker's point as he or she shares it, by writing along the line. It is a good idea to try to use your partner's words if possible, but the key is to try and boil the whole thing down to a manageable length.

Step 4: If you are the listener, when finished summarising, you should check to make sure that you have captured what your partner meant. If not, listen again and change it until the speaker knows that you understand.

Often communication goes wrong because words in our 'fan of reference' do not mean exactly the same as words in the other person's 'fan of reference'. We think we know what they mean, but we are mistaken. It is important to do a meaning check with each point as it is summarised along a spoke of the wheel.

Step 5: Draw another spoke out from the centre and summarise the next point along it. Keep doing this with each new point that your partner raises until he or she has talked out every aspect of that point. Do not try to comment at this stage, but simply aim to understand what your partner is wanting to communicate.

If you need to ask a question to clarify something, that's okay, but limit your speaking to simply that — clarifying!

Step 6: As your spouse shares on a point, there may be several aspects to that one point. You should diagram these sub-points by drawing branches off that spoke and writing along each branch.

Step 7: Keep mapping what is being shared until your partner has completely finished all he or she wants to say about the topic! Then change roles.

Step 8: When both of you have completely finished sharing (and being listened to and mapped), look over the two maps that represent the two points of view on the topic. Usually, about twenty per cent of the points are really important. It helps convey even more understanding if each of you indicates priorities on your map by putting #1 alongside the most important point, #2 alongside the next and so on.

Step 9: *Use highlighters to bring out even more under-standing of each other's viewpoint.* For example, one colour might be used to highlight points that you both agree on. Another colour might be used to highlight any points about which some constructive action can be taken. The use of colour on your maps will help you understand even more of what is going on in each of you in relation to this topic.

Step 10: *If action needs to be taken, choose something that both of you are comfortable with.* This may involve some give and take at times.

The first benefit of this structured approach to working through a conflict is that it can be easily learned. Although the list of ten steps might seem a little daunting, the approach seems to work almost magically, right from the start.

One reason for this is that much of the heat in a conflict comes from the feeling that 'I'm not being listened to'! This mapping process forces each of you to listen to your spouse closely — more closely than you would ever normally listen. Your husband or wife knows that he or she will be heard and this takes away some of the pressure that usually exists in a conflict to force the other person to take notice by turning up the volume, using violent words or some other tactic.

Conflicts arise out of the clash of two powerful sets of needs. The fear that drives the conflict and causes it to escalate is the fear that 'my needs won't be met'. While mapping does not guarantee that all of the needs you both have will be met, it does ensure that the *first* need, the need to be listened to, is met. It also provides a simple structure that enables the intensity of emotions to be controlled so that they don't block reaching a constructive solution to your conflict.

FIONA'S MAP OF TERRY'S POINT OF VIEW

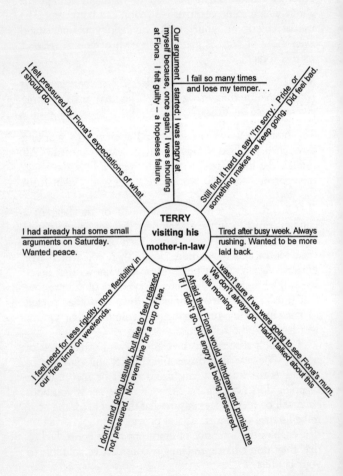

TERRY visiting his mother-in-law

Our argument started: I was angry at myself because, once again, I was shouting at Fiona. I felt guilty – a hopeless failure.

I fail so many times and lose my temper. . .

Still find it hard to say 'I'm sorry'. Pride or something makes me keep going. Did feel bad.

I felt pressured by Fiona's expectations of what I should do.

I had already had some small arguments on Saturday. Wanted peace.

Tired after busy week. Always rushing. Wanted to be more laid back.

I feel need for less rigidity, more flexibility in our free time on weekends.

I don't mind going usually, but like to feel relaxed and not pressured. Not even time for a cup of tea.

Afraid that Fiona would withdraw and punish me if I didn't go, but angry at being pressured.

I wasn't sure if we were going to see Fiona's mum. We don't always go. Hadn't talked about this this morning.

TERRY'S MAP OF FIONA'S POINT OF VIEW

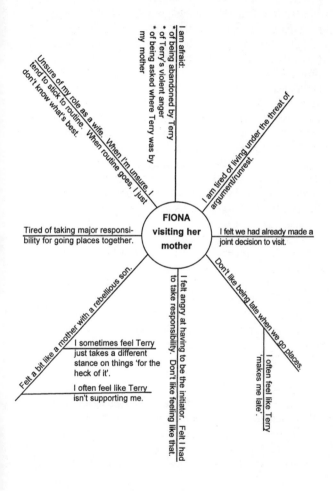

I am afraid:
* of being abandoned by Terry
* of Terry's violent anger
* of being asked where Terry was by my mother

I am tired of living under the threat of argument/unrest.

Unsure of my role as a wife. When I'm unsure, I tend to stick to routine. When routine goes, I just don't know what's best.

FIONA visiting her mother

Tired of taking major responsibility for going places together.

I felt we had already made a joint decision to visit.

Felt a bit like a mother with a rebellious son.

I sometimes feel Terry just takes a different stance on things 'for the heck of it'.

I often feel like Terry isn't supporting me.

I felt angry at having to be the initiator. Felt I had to take responsibility. Don't like feeling like that.

Don't like being late when we go places.

I often feel like Terry 'makes me late'.

When Terry and Fiona did their first mapping exercise, they chose to re-work an argument from the previous week. They had clashed badly over the issue of a visit to Fiona's mother's place on Sunday morning. Often on a Sunday morning, they would go over to have morning tea with Fiona's mother who was in a nursing home.

This Sunday, Terry had got up late and Fiona felt pressured because they were going to be too late for morning tea. Feelings escalated, Terry shouted at Fiona and Fiona ended up driving off to see her mother on her own, leaving Terry seething with anger. The day was a write-off and they felt so bad about their anger at each other that neither of them could face going to church that night.

They resumed talking on Monday, but it took another day or so before they felt comfortable with each other. They had not talked through their thoughts and feelings at all. They had simply put the conflict aside and tried to be nice to each other. It seemed like a good situation to practise mapping on!

The maps they produced, as they listened to each other, are diagrammed in Figure 1 and Figure 2.

Usually, if a conflict is over an issue that both partners feel strongly about, there will be a significant release of emotion accompanying the first few points with mapping. This doesn't mean that the first speaker *shouts* the first few points, but there is a noticeable intensity to the way he or she speaks.

Without the structure of mapping, the partner would also be trying to get his or her point of view across with emotional intensity. And that would normally lead to an escalation in volume, with no-one really listening and little hope of working through the conflict in any constructive way.

With mapping, you can literally *hear* a point of change in the intensity of each person's presentation. A moment comes when the anger/hostility/fear, or whatever the dominant emotion is, suddenly drops away and the speaker is noticeably calmer.

Why does this happen? Two reasons. The first is that the speaker has had a chance to release some of that emotion in talking his or her viewpoint out. The second is that he or she feels listened to. Somehow, even if we don't agree, I can't feel so angry when I know that you have listened to me.

Mapping provides a structure that enables you to work through a conflict without damaging your partner. And the process contains within it the seeds of healing, as emotions are released and each of you feels listened to.

As Terry and Fiona did the mapping exercise in my office, you could 'hear' the emotion drain away. It was almost as though, for the first time, they had really listened to each other — and each one felt listened to! At the end of their mapping, we spent a moment looking at the priorities for each of them. They numbered, according to strength, the three most powerful factors working in them at the time of the argument.

Then they talked. For each of them, it seemed almost a new experience to try to understand the other's point of view, but the raw emotion was gone and they gave themselves to the task. I asked them to address the question, 'What can we do so that this sort of problem doesn't happen again?' They quickly settled on the need to talk something over ahead of time so that they were not just working on assuming.

Terry seemed to be a bit surprised that Fiona was happy to have a more flexible weekend; and they tried to work out some ideas so that Terry would take a bit more of the load when they agreed to do something. Terry responded to Fiona's comments about being unsure of her role as a wife by saying: 'But that's exactly how I feel about being your husband! Often I don't know what the right thing is and I think that's when I explode my worst. A lot of it is frustration at myself.'

Fiona decided that, since it was her mum they were visiting, she would be happy to try to get up a little bit earlier and make sure that Terry had at least a cup of tea before they went. She also seemed to be helped by Terry's statement that he did feel bad when he lost his temper and that he really regretted it, even if he found it too hard to say 'sorry'.

They left, feeling a lot more confident that, if they used mapping next time an argument began, they could head off a lot of the hurt they had experienced in the past. They also had an assignment to practise by mapping any differences or disagreements during the coming week.

Over the next couple of months, Terry and Fiona became competent at mapping — and, more importantly, at handling hassles well! Although progress was marked by some more 'failures', they saw themselves getting better — and they kept going. Their marriage strengthened and they felt progressively more able to affirm and build each other in love.

✠ Further practical ways to handle hassles
Here are a number of additional practical ways to manage conflict well:

1. *Don't just ignore conflict and disagreement*
Often when two 'stuffers' disagree, the approach used will be to try to ignore the conflict, hoping that it will magically disappear. It rarely does. More commonly, the anger ferments inside and is added to each time a new disagreement occurs. Then it becomes bitterness, which flavours every aspect of the marriage, leaving both partners cold and distant.

While it may not be necessary to map every conflict

or even to talk through every conflict in a detailed way, the disagreement needs to be recognised and talked out at least to the point where reconciliation is reached. Ignoring tends to leave us stewing with anger long after the sun has gone down.

2. *Control the intensity of your emotions!*
It *is* possible to control anger. Many people, when they are angry, do not want to acknowledge this. They feel they have a right to explode with anger. However, as we have already seen, anger expressed in verbal violence damages the security in a marriage relationship. It is important that we learn more mature, less destructive ways of expressing it.

Obviously, mapping is a helpful technique here. It provides a structure to help you 'be slow to become angry'. Sometimes you may need to take a time out, a period of an hour or two, to cool down. It helps to walk or do something active during the time out. Adrenalin is burnt up and you feel a little more mellowed; that means more control over the intensity of your emotions when you talk things through.

3. *Take responsibility for your functioning in relationship*
As normal humans, we tend to avoid taking responsibility for any of our less worthy behaviour. This 'shifting the blame' is as old as the Garden of Eden. The husband who blames his wife for *causing* his anger may fool himself, but he doesn't fool anyone else. We are all responsible for our own actions and decisions.

The message is clear. Whether someone has wronged us or we have wronged someone else, we need to take responsibility for taking steps to sort it out. We are *never* in a position to be able to say: 'Well, it's not my fault, so I don't have to do anything.' We can never avoid the obligation to take personal responsibility for our choices and actions. And often that will mean taking the initiative for sorting through some conflict or disagreement.

4. *Watch your language*

Time after time, in marriage conflicts, damaging words are used. The wife shouts at her husband: 'You're an idiot!' The husband lashes at his wife: 'You stupid bitch!' Foul language is thrown, and the spirit of each partner is lacerated and torn by the words.

Nothing justifies this. We have to control our use of language. Otherwise, we pay a price in the lack of safety and intimacy we experience in our marriage. We can never overestimate the damage potential of our words.

In this regard, it is important to avoid the use of 'buzz-words' when we are seeking to work through a conflict. Buzz-words include words that are over-emotive, that exaggerate or that, in some ways, provoke hostility. Some of the most common buzz-words include 'always' and 'never': 'You *always* ignore my mother!', 'You *never* keep the house tidy!'

These words escalate the level of the conflict, because the receiver knows he or she is being unfairly clobbered!

But husbands and wives sometimes have pet buzz-words — ones they have learned over the years that have unique wounding effects for their spouse. He calls her 'Porky' (she is overweight); she calls him 'motormouth' (he talks a lot). The message of these kinds of words is always hurtful. For the sake of your marriage, press the 'delete' button on them!

5. *Stay focussed on the present situation*

Any time that we haul up the past to get more fire-power to wound the person we are in conflict with, we escalate the conflict. We need to put the past behind us in these situations and forgive each other. We should never bring it up again in the present in order to win an argument. We will always do better in resolving conflict if we stay focussed on the specific situation that has provoked the conflict and not bring other issues in to muddy the water.

6. *Forgive. . . and forgive again*
This is so important a point that we will focus a whole chapter on what it means to forgive. However, in relation. to handling conflict well, we will do well to remind ourselves that we are to continue extending forgiveness, with no limit!

This is tough, but nothing else does so much in restoring relationship that has been damaged in conflict.

*   *   *

Let us put the ideas in this chapter together. Conflict is not always a negative process. The truth is, often our love can deepen for our marriage partner as we work through our differences well.

But conflict also has the potential to destroy love. When we use 'dirty tactics', when we let our emotions escalate with no control, when winning becomes more important than loving — then our marriage is at risk!

However, when we make use of good conflict management skills — when we listen and seek to understand each other's point of view, when we forgive past hurts and work at solving disagreements with a joint problem-solving approach — then, we discover that conflicts can lead to positive growth.

The truth is, handled well, conflicts frequently lead to the *most* valuable growth-steps that we can take in our marriages.

Questions for thought and discussion

✠ PERSONAL INVENTORY

One of the benefits of not marrying is that you have much greater freedom to do things 'my way'! Once we marry, we put ourselves in the situation of having to work through to 'our way' of doing and thinking. And that is not always an easy process.

Personal insecurity (and do we hate to face this!) is usually what forces us to fight and argue so strongly for the rightness of 'my viewpoint'. Personal insecurity drives us to demand our way; personal insecurity drives us to criticise our partner's way or their opinion.

Ironically, the most dominating among us, the ones who insist and have to control, thereby only succeed in demonstrating the depth of their own sense of inferiority. It looks so different to the inferiority feelings of the 'doormat' person, but it's all the same when you lift the lid a little. It's the insecurity of the person who can't afford to be wrong!

But, of course, marriage is worthwhile and we can learn fruitful ways of working out the inevitable differences we will have. And the truth is that, in learning to do this well, we grow. But it often requires some thoughtful self-analysis and a determination to let God make changes in our functioning where this is necessary.

1. Drawing on the concept of 'puffers' and 'stuffers', how do I see my characteristic way of handling my anger in disagreements with my spouse? Am I more of a 'puffer', or a 'stuffer'?

2. To what extent do I treat my partner like an enemy when we conflict over something? Why am I like this?

3. How important is it for me to win arguments with my spouse? Where does this insecurity in me come from?

4. What, specifically, do I tend to do with my anger whenever a conflict situation comes up with my spouse? What does my spouse do?

5. To what extent am I able to listen to my spouse when we conflict? To what extent do I talk 'over' him/her, trying to force my viewpoint through?

6. What blocks me from being a better listener when I am having a disagreement with my partner?

7. Which of the further practical ways of handling hassles, outlined in this chapter, is most relevant to me and my handling disagreements better? Why is this the most important for me?

✠ SHARING WITH YOUR PARTNER
Review together the ten steps involved in mapping. Discuss these and make sure that you have a clear understanding of what is involved and can follow the steps.

Now, choose an incident (for example, the argument we had on the way to work last Monday) that you have recently disagreed over. Decide who will begin sharing and who will begin mapping and proceed to listen to everything each of you wants to say on the topic. When you have finished, talk over the benefits of this approach.

Set yourselves the task of catching a conflict before it develops this coming week. At the first indications, agree to map your viewpoints — and see how much better it goes!

✠ GROUP WORK
Tani and Roger have been married three years. Their biggest arguments happen over money matters. Typically, Roger becomes abusive and tells Tani that she is a 'spendthrift' and that they'll never have any savings if she keeps on.

Tani's usual approach is to accuse Roger of being a 'miser', of never showing any generosity since their wedding day. She has a sharp tongue and usually outguns him pretty quickly, with the result that he withdraws. They never apologise for their ungracious behaviour to each other, and they don't seem able to resolve this issue.

8. What are the things that you can see that Tani and Roger are doing wrong?

9. What are the dangers for them as a result of this failure to work the issue through?

10. What changes would the group suggest they try? Have someone record these ideas and, as a group, list the ideas in order of priority.

11. What do you think of the principle of trying to sort out disagreements 'before the sun goes down'?

12. What practical steps have you found helpful in handling disagreements so that they are not destructive?

13. Share a conflict or disagreement in your marriage that had a positive outcome because of the way it was handled.

14. What generalised words (e.g. 'always', 'never') does each couple in the group use that needs to be avoided? Discuss tactics to ensure such dangerous words can be eliminated.

9

Forgive one another

'YOU HAVE GOT TO BE JOKING! I could never forgive him, not if he begged me for a thousand years. After all he's done, he can rot in hell!'

These were angry words — words that were fuelled by years of loneliness and pain. The words came in response to a friend's question: 'Kathy, have you ever forgiven Paul?' Kathy's intense reaction showed that forgiveness just wasn't on the agenda at all.

There was a long history behind this reaction. Paul and Kathy had been happily married and were raising a daughter, paying off a mortgage and working in a new business partnership. During the early months of the business, Paul was required to travel interstate on several occasions. On each occasion, he would call and let Kathy know his schedule, contact phone number and other details of what he was involved in.

On one occasion, Paul gave Kathy a number to call if she needed him while he was away. Paul gave it to her off the top of his head from memory. Kathy recorded the number, but didn't need to use it at the time. On a much later trip, the number Paul gave her was not answering, so she called the number given to her on the earlier occasion. The female voice on the other end of the phone said she hadn't seen Paul for a few weeks, but that he was expected soon.

Paul rang home that evening and Kathy confronted him about the identity of the female on the other end of the line. The conversation became a long argument with many claims and counter claims. When it was all clarified, it was evident that on Kathy's interstate trips, he was indeed doing business, but was also spending an additional day or two with a former girlfriend whose number he had never written down but memorised, only to inadvertently give it out on the earlier occasion mentioned.

This was six years ago. Paul had been quick to give up his mistress and did his business by phone until he could employ an agent. He said he was sorry, but Kathy was too hurt to extend any forgiveness, so the relationship languished between total hostility and truce.

Not all marriages experience betrayal and pain at the depth of Paul and Kathy's, but many do, some even surpassing the depth of theirs. And the question of forgiveness is always relevant. Forgiveness is a key factor in any relationship and especially one as close as a marriage.

The closer two people are in relationship, the greater the benefits from intimacy. But it is also true that the closer two people are, the greater the hurt caused by betrayal or breaches of trust. A couple who are open and trusting will always be more devastated by betrayal of trust than a couple who have never developed much depth or trust in their relationship.

No matter what the condition of a marriage, forgiveness always has an important place. Unfortunately, as in the case of Paul and Kathy's marriage, there is often an unwillingness to consider the possibility of forgiving, as the drive for revenge is so intense that the benefits of forgiving seem to pale into insignificance. It is also important to know that people often do not have a very clear sense of what it means to forgive.

Two factors — an unwilling spirit and an uninformed mind — constitute major barriers to both the restoration of a broken marriage and to growth in an unbroken marriage.

✠ Blockages to forgiveness

One of the key blockages to letting go of grudges or hurts caused by a spouse is that some self-styled experts believe forgiving is either unnecessary or serves as a sign of weakness. They pass this message on. If we accept their message without thinking it through or without really understanding what forgiving involves and why it is important to do it, then we forego the possibility of healing for ourselves and for our relationships.

Unashamedly and unequivocally, we believe that the capacity to forgive is absolutely essential to all human relationships. If we cannot overlook faults in one another, even grievous faults such as adultery, then we are not well-equipped to handle this body-contact sport which we call life. People are imperfect, ourselves included. We all fail at some points. We need to be able to extend forgiveness to others and also to ask for forgiveness when we fail others. If we cannot do these things, then we are destined to a lot of excess loneliness in life.

This is not to minimise the enormity of hurts such as adultery. Notwithstanding the liberated, trendy view occasionally put about on this issue, cheating on your spouse *destroys* relationship because it destroys trust. We do not minimise this sort of damage. We simply say that, if forgiveness is sought and given (not necessarily immediately), then marriages can be rebuilt and rise even stronger out of the rubble.

Many couples do not really understand what forgiveness involves. Some want to forgive, but get confused when resentment seems to continue even after they have said the words of forgiveness. Others, trapped in unhappy alliances, have their lives devastated by anger and bitterness, without ever fully understanding what is going on and how forgiveness could so dramatically change the picture.

An understanding of forgiveness is important. Once the process of forgiving one another is understood, then at least choices about what to do can be made with correct information. We don't have to respond simply out of unexamined emotional reflexes.

But before we talk in more detail about what forgiveness is, we need to clear out another blockage. Many people confuse forgiveness with reconciliation. Reconciliation is the restoring of the relationship, putting things back to the way they were before, trusting and relating as though the offence never happened.

Such a huge step is more than forgiveness. There are some situations where the renewing of the relationship is not wise or warranted. We are in agreement in our counselling practices that actions such as repeats of adultery or physical abuse in a marriage ought not to be followed by reconciliation or getting back together, though we certainly allow that possibility if there is demonstrated evidence of change in the offender over time. But even with hurts as big as these, we still believe forgiveness is relevant, even if the renewing of the relationship is not.

No, forgiveness is not the same as reconciliation. Sometimes, it is quite possible to forgive someone for the wrongs done to you and yet not have any ongoing relationship with them. To do so might be simply too distressing.

Reconciliation is a process, a considerable journey. Forgiveness is really only the first step that might make the journey of reconciliation possible, where this is wise.

Well, what is forgiveness? How do I really forgive?

How do I know if someone is really sorry? These are some of the common questions people raise.

In response to the question 'What is forgiveness?', David Augsburger says:

Forgiveness is. . . *rare*
hard and
costly.

This seems to give the question some important perspective. It doesn't tell us what it is, or even how we achieve it, but it reminds us that we are dealing with a real life issue and that we cannot microwave an answer. Central to our understanding is the fact that forgiveness is costly. But back to the question.

✠ What is forgiveness?

In essence, forgiveness is giving up the desire for revenge, giving up the desire to pay the other person back.

In our humanness, whenever someone wrongs us, we experience at least two emotions. First of all, we feel hurt: 'That's not fair, I didn't deserve that,' we think. Next — and this may come so fast that we don't really experience the hurt — we feel angry: 'How dare you do that to me. I'll get you!' are the sorts of thoughts that go through our minds. Some part of us would dearly love revenge, would love to see our spouse paid back for what he or she has done to wound us.

When we forgive our spouse, we 'let them off the hook'. It is not often an easy thing to do.

We get scared. We think, 'If I forgive him or her, they'll think it didn't hurt me. They'll think they can do it again.' Often, we hang onto our unforgiveness because we aren't prepared to take the risk. Unforgiveness serves both to pay the other person back and to protect us from the risk of more hurt. The trouble with unforgiveness is that, although it serves as excellent protection, it makes for lousy future intimacy. When we hang onto unforgiveness, we take the risk of settling for increased isolation in our future.

Kathy wasn't prepared to forgive Paul. He was going to pay and pay and pay. While she still felt pain, Kathy was going to expect Paul to keep paying. The trouble with this approach is that there is no end to this vengeance-seeking. Forgiveness means wiping the debt.

It is really hard for us to take this route. If our spouse comes home late, embarrasses us in front of others, puts us down or fails us in some way, we tend to want to make them pay. We find subtle or direct ways of seeking vengeance.

Kathy did this with Paul. She was determined not to let him off the hook. Her words and her actions towards him ensured that she was not going to try to wipe the slate clean. She wanted him to pay, so she worked at reminding him of his infidelity and stopped all warm communication. If, instead, she had worked through the difficult task of forgiving him, then she and Paul might have had a chance of rebuilding the marriage. He was remorseful, but she wouldn't let the debt be settled.

Who loses in a situation like this? Both marriage partners! But that's not fair; it was his fault! True, but he has done what he can to express his regret at his action: he has changed his behaviour and wants the marriage to continue. The ball is in Kathy's court. If she will not forgive, then both continue to suffer the consequences. If she does forgive, accepting the cost herself and freeing Paul from further payment, then the marriage at least has a chance of being renewed in love and trust once again.

But what if Paul had not been remorseful? What if he wanted his marriage and his mistress — and played some game to try to keep both? This is a different situation.

This would be a time for a tough decision. Where a man tries to have a wife and a mistress, we could not realistically expect the marriage to work. Probably, Kathy would have to give Paul an ultimatum and live with the consequences of that decision. But even then, she would be best served if she worked her way through to forgiving him, even though the marriage was over! A statement like that almost sounds ridiculous, so we need to explain what we mean.

✠ Why should we forgive?

Ultimately, we need to forgive for selfish reasons. Forgiveness always feels like it's for the other person — and certainly they do benefit when forgiveness is given.

But the truth is that we need to forgive, or we simply end up hurting ourselves more. The person who will not forgive holds onto bitterness inside and, like a poison, it does its work of souring the spirit of that person. Anger and resentment nurtured within, even towards someone whose actions justify our anger and resentment, breed a slow poison that affects us.

And, even when we do not recognise it, others do. It is a law of the spirit that we take that poison with us: it intrudes into other relationships and into other areas of our lives. That is why we need to forgive.

An unforgiving spirit in any of us is not conducive to well-being, either emotional or physical. A person consumed with anger and revenge-seeking creates havoc within his or her various internal systems. Research supports the claim that holding grudges and anger reduces essential brain chemicals, resulting in depressive moods and generally poor functioning of emotions.

Most wives can testify that when they are upset with

their husbands they cannot eat well, or digest food properly. Similarly, husbands testify to acid stomach and upset bowel routines when their anger at their spouse is not resolved.

One study, based on the Simonton's research with cancer patients, identified four traits characteristic of those prone to develop cancer. This study by Achterberg, Matthews and Simonton in 1976 and published in *Psychotherapy: Theory, Research and Practice* found that the first trait was 'a great tendency to hold resentment and a marked inability to forgive'.

Of course, this neither means that every person with cancer must have held onto resentment, nor does it imply that every person who holds onto unforgiveness will get cancer. But it is an intriguing finding, suggesting at least that the likelihood of certain forms of cancer may be increased if we will not forgive. The risk to our physical, emotional and spiritual health is the reason that forgiving our spouse and others, including ourselves, is not an optional extra.

There is, of course, another reason for practising forgiveness towards our spouse in the ongoing journey of marriage. This reason is simply a recognition that, in our imperfection, we will need their forgiveness at times, too. How can we expect our failings to be overlooked if we will not extend mercy to our partner?

✠ How does forgiveness take place?
What is the process of forgiveness? Husbands and wives often wonder how long it will take to forgive.

The answer here depends on a number of factors. The first one is: *How clear are we on the details of what has occurred?* Until we are sure of the facts, it is hard for us to move towards resolution. We usually need to know *what* we are forgiving in order to actually forgive.

The second factor is: *How prepared are we to acknow-ledge that wrong has been done?* We need to say, without denial, 'It's true, my spouse wronged me.' Too often, we fall into the trap of saying, 'Forget it. It's nothing really', when deep inside we have been deeply hurt. Similarly, the party doing the wrong needs to admit it. Discounting an offence or denying its painfulness blocks off our expe-riencing pain and also blocks off full forgiveness towards the offender. So it is important to admit the reality.

Until these two preliminary events occur, resolution is partial at best. We cannot bring about change until we admit the need. Once there is admission of offence and hurt, then progress in the work of forgiving becomes possible. We are ready then to move onto the third factor.

The third factor is: *How willing am I to give up any idea of revenge?* This involves an inward resolution of the spirit. Frequently, it is helpful to do this before a coun-sellor. Many people find it makes it a more significant moment to make this resolution in the form of a prayer before God, asking for his help in living the forgiveness out.

Some counsellors believe this process should be imme-diate. However, most people cannot arrive at it so swiftly. To assume they can is to put undue pressure on them. Kathy could mouth the necessary words under pressure, but there would have been no real ownership of her pain. Deep hurts need to be owned by the hurting person before they can move to the point of forgiving and this usually takes some time and a listening, caring friend or counsellor.

It is also important to understand that this process does not mean that we will automatically forget about the hurt. The truth is that, as humans, we will continue to remem-ber. Every now and then, a thought will pop into our minds or something will trigger the memory and the incident will again be there! We will feel again the knot in our stomach and the force of the hurt. We will still feel the anger: 'How could he have done that?'; 'Why did she treat me that way?'

The fourth factor is: *How do I cope with continued bad memories after I have forgiven?* These are not indications that we have failed to forgive properly. Rather, they simply mean that we are normal people. That's how normal people function. The first thing, then, is to be thankful for our normality. The second is to take this fresh opportunity to renew within our hearts our affirmation of forgiveness. Over time, we will notice that the memory and the emotion will dissipate, but it takes a long time.

Bob and Jill were two who were able to do the tough work of moving through forgiveness to rebuild their marriage.

Bob was a punter and, over several years, became indebted to several bookmakers for large sums of money. The family car, home and savings were all lost in due course. Jill couldn't handle the betrayal and anguish and became hospitalised for severe depression. At this point, with the collapse of all that was dear to him staring him in the face, Bob acknowledged his needs. He finally admitted his addiction, sought professional help and began recovery. Jill made good progress, forgave Bob and they began to rebuild their shattered relationship.

But Bob kept sabotaging it. He felt such shame, guilt and regret for what he had done that he would not let himself get close to Jill again — and no amount of assurance from Jill could get him past the hurdle.

Bob had to forgive himself — but he couldn't. He knew Jill forgave him, but he still felt unworthy. His problem is not unlike that of many people who honestly face what they have done and can't get past it. Two lengthy counselling sessions followed and, during those sessions, Bob came to understand the following truths:

1. It was healthy and appropriate for him to regret what had occurred.
2. Not permitting himself to fail and demanding perfection of himself was tantamount to playing God — and also setting himself up for further failure.
3. Discounting the forgiveness given by Jill was a distortion of his own importance and amounted to a kind of inverted pride.

It wasn't long before Bob saw he didn't have to be perfect to be accepted and that it was because he was too fearful about possible failure again that he clung to the failure that had already occurred. Bob also saw that by being so fearful and refusing to forgive himself, he was daily adding pain to Jill. This was certainly not what he wanted. Slowly, he came to accept the forgiveness that Jill offered and they were able to rebuild.

Bob's situation raises another point worth pondering. When we know we need to ask for forgiveness, we need to do so knowing that, for the other person to forgive us, *they* must bear the pain and release us. Bob did want to be close to Jill again, but he also feared that he couldn't trust Jill to release him fully.

So, asking for forgiveness is not a 'simple' solution. It is a costly route. And yet the cost is never as great as the cost of denying our guilt, or refusing to seek or give forgiveness.

✠ What place has forgiveness in irretrievable marriage breakdown?

There are times, of course, when the actions of one partner are so damaging to the marriage that it cannot be saved. Repetitions of physical abuse of a spouse, repetitions of adultery, a pattern of chronic deception, a spouse caught in addiction who resists seeking help, serious criminal behaviour, a partner found to be sexually abusing a child in the family — actions such as these are so damaging to the marriage base of trust and loving intimacy that frequently the 'innocent' partner is unable to contemplate a continuation of the marriage.

While no-one *wants* to break the marriage in the sense that it is seen as desirable, it is sometimes, nevertheless, the lesser of two evils. We need to acknowledge again that our actions have consequences and that some actions are so hurtful that they make it unwise, perhaps virtually impossible, for a marriage partner to consider going on in the marriage.

Does forgiveness have a place in situations such as this? We believe it does. Without being simplistic or trite, we believe that the person who carries their hurt away from the marriage and continues to define their life over the remaining years by attitudes of anger, resentment and bitterness, chooses a self-destructive pathway. While forgiveness, in this case, certainly does *not* mean continuing the marriage, it still is a journey that the person needs to take. It will not be easy — it may take years to feel like 'I've finally gotten over the hurt' — but it is important to begin.

Forgiveness in this situation will largely be an interior journey of letting go of the bitterness, probably not outwardly expressed to the offending partner. However, the covert, inner journey will be evident in the person's ongoing life. He or she will relate to the offending person, if they have to have ongoing contact, in ways that attempt to be gracious, rather than from a stance of seeking revenge. He or she will seek to move on in life, making the best of tough times, looking for positives, working to build a fulfilling future, rather than being consumed with bitterness and regret.

The alternative to this approach simply does not work well for anyone — the innocent party, the offender, children, wider family or friends.

✠ What place has forgiveness in all marriages?

The examples we have used in this chapter involve serious breaches and hurts within the marriage relationship. Forgiveness is especially costly in such situations, but nothing else will give hope for a way ahead.

Much of the time, however, the issue of forgiveness is really about overlooking the little hurts and faults we find in each other. If we harbour grudges, instead of working things through, talking hurts out and letting go, we carry the seeds of destruction in our way of relating.

Forgiveness is not a luxury item in a marriage. Every fulfilling marriage does so because the partners have learned this secret. They practise in big or small ways, living in forgiveness.

Questions for thought and discussion

The 'three little words' that actually make a marriage work are not 'I love you', but 'please forgive me'. This chapter has explored the difficulty we have in actually forgiving each other and how destructive that can be.

David Augsburger's statement that forgiveness is hard, rare and costly is verified daily in our clinical experience. This we find is mainly due to unwilling hearts and uninformed minds. Those who do choose to 'give up any desire to pay back' find the difficulty in the decision offset by the freedom and growth in relationship they gain.

✠ PERSONAL INVENTORY

1. You have read our definition of forgiveness. Now, make up one of your own that expresses what you believe is the key emphasis.

2. What is your most common emotional reaction when you feel wronged?

3. What was the most painful betrayal you have experienced? How have you dealt with the need to forgive?

4. [Men:] How would you respond if Paul was your best friend and he came to you for advice? [Women:] How would you advise Kathy? [For both:] Imagine that the roles were reversed and Paul was wronged by Kathy. What response would you now give to your respective friends? Does it differ markedly?

5. What do you need to forgive yourself for and what is blocking you from doing so?

✠ SHARING WITH YOUR PARTNER

Discuss with each other your responses to Paul and Kathy's situation. Share your feelings towards each of them.

Each choose an incident from your own marriage that has caused you pain. Share it with one another without comment. (This may be threatening, but an essential step to living in forgiveness.)

Then each share where you believe you are along the road to forgiveness. (Do this with the help of the 'How does forgiveness take place?' section.)

✠ GROUP WORK

Have someone read aloud the profile of Bob and Jill and then address the following questions:

6. Why might Jill not have acted sooner to do something about the situation?

7. In what ways could Bob's feelings have kept him from getting close to Jill?

8. What might Jill have been feeling when her forgiveness seemed to be rejected by Bob?

9. If Bob was a member of your group, how could you all help him through his feelings of guilt and shame?

10. How has each group member dealt with unforgiveness? Share experiences.

10

Have lots of fun

MOST PEOPLE ENJOY THE CHANCE for relaxation and
fun. When couples are first going out and getting to
know each other, it's more often than not in a context
of fun activities. But, by the time they are married, this
important aspect of living often gets put aside. Balance
is so often lost when cares and responsibilities take over.

✠ Why we need fun in marriage
It's now generally agreed that for any marriage to remain
healthy and growing, it needs to have some fun in it.
Also, healthy people cannot usually remain that way
without a good balance of fun and laughter in their lives.
It's been suggested that having fun, relaxing and laughing
are natural antidotes to sadness and depression.

In marriages where fun is shared, even greater benefits
can be provided. Having fun can act in the relationship
to provide relief from unresolved conflicts and built-up
pressures. Sharing fun also helps improve conditions for
dealing with them. Relaxed fun acts like a cleansing tonic
for anxious, overwhelmed minds and weary bodies — it
can help to wash out the poisons of anxiety, fear and
tension.

Sometimes, we have been able to help struggling couples look into this area of their marriage by asking: 'What

do you two do to have fun together?' It's a good question every couple needs to face from time to time.

Marriage is a serious business; we cannot deny that. The task of bringing two lives together and learning all the skills needed to develop intimacy is no small task. As we've already seen, it involves a lot of input developing good communication skills; learning to forgive and accept each other; and working out ways of handling disagreements and conflicts so they don't ruin the closeness we've built up. It means learning to compromise, learning to give up some of what we want in any situation in order to express our love to our spouse — and so much more. Finding time for sharing fun helps make all this easier.

And, as we learn to do all this, we will also be learning to keep everything in balance and not take ourselves too seriously. We need to build fun into our marriages. I emphasise the word 'build'. It needs not only spontaneity, but planning.

How does this happen? We need to take initiatives, because fun will not always just happen. The chances are that if we just let things go and hope that fun and laughter will automatically flow in our marriages, we will be on a downward slope. Pressures of work, financial demands, the children and 'deep and meaningful' relationship issues are most likely to squeeze the fun right out. We need to plan fun times.

The good times, the times of relaxation and laughter, don't all need to register '10' on the Richter Scale of Pleasure. Low-key pleasant events are fine. It doesn't matter if they only register a '2'!

Everyone is a deposit in the 'bank' of our marriage relationship, building up the balance into healthy proportions. If the deposits are regular, then when we hit the tough times in our marriage (and let's face it, every marriage does hit some hard times), we then have something to draw on. If we have not built in our fun times, if we don't have much in the bank of goodwill in our relationship then, when tough times hit, it's easy to find ourselves wondering why we're in this marriage.

Think about those couples and families you know where fun and laughter are absent, where the closest you get to a smile is a nod of recognition. Think of marriages where complaints always supplant thanks, and gratitude or praise seldom figure in the conversation. Because fun is absent and laughter is often of the hollow kind, everything seems dull and boring.

Such a marriage has no vibrancy; there just seems to be no life left in it.

✠ What a marriage without fun is like: a case study

Take the Freeman boys, for example. All five were raised never to show any emotion. Their parents told them that was 'sissy'. So they always hid their sadness and disappointments — even their joys. All of them have been married for many years, but their restricted emotions have meant at least two of these marriages have been in trouble.

So, when the eldest of them, Steve, now an accountant, informed us in counselling one day that he didn't know what his wife Gina enjoyed doing for fun and recreation, we enquired more deeply about his family and his upbringing.

It seemed Steve and his brothers were seldom affirmed and never shared fun or enjoyed games as children with either parent. 'We were always told what we did wrong and were punished for it. That was not so bad. It was just that we didn't get taken out and allowed to have fun, because we had to be quiet. So we just read and talked among ourselves. When we could get away with it, we played a few ball games outside with each other, but I'm sure our parents didn't approve — and they never joined in, anyway.'

It was, therefore, no surprise that Steve seldom took Gina out or enjoyed relaxing with her. He found it difficult to laugh unless he was cynical or sarcastic — and this usually was at her expense.

Further questioning revealed this was the usual pattern among the Freeman males. Women and girls were not usually included in any of their activities. Their learned 'macho' attitudes meant that when a female dared to offer an opinion or join in the conversation, they would only smile cynically or make a snide comment to each other.

Steve had thus entered marriage with cynical attitudes to women generally and totally unaware of his wife's needs. He seemed quite ignorant of the importance of providing a balance of fun and pleasure to keep his marriage alive and enjoyable. It was little wonder Gina thought he had a 'warped sense of humour'. She had been hurt by it too many times. Now, having accepted nearly twenty-five years of lacklustre marriage, it was not surprising that Gina was expressing her disappointment.

Their three children had also lost out. Rather than being enjoyed and made to feel special by their father, they had been mostly tolerated or just blandly accepted. These attitudes compounded many other problems for the children. Not only had this marriage lost its spark, but it seemed there was very little being done by Steve to maintain Gina's interest. With little joy, no 'fun' and no spirit left in the relationship, everything was stale, empty. To inject life and hope, something needed to be done urgently.

Tearfully, almost despairingly, Gina said, 'We've really just been going through the motions for years. How can

I get Steve to show his emotions and understand we need to enjoy life a lot more? I can't remember a time when we last had any fun together!'

This was said more to her husband than to us. But, as an appeal, it was met with apparently cold indifference. As we watched her tears, we sadly realised this was a case of almost too late. Yet, even as we listened, I also sensed there might be something that could save this devastated and impoverished marriage.

'Life wasn't meant to be all serious hard work!' I said. 'It's really quite okay to take time to enjoy life. In fact, taking time out having fun is very therapeutic. You don't ever have to feel guilty taking time for relaxation and fun — it's positively good for you.'

This was clearly unfamiliar news to the workaholic accountant who sat before us. He'd been taught by both a controlling, unfeeling mother and a hard 'macho' father that life was tough and always unremitting. As for having fun, expressing joy and other positive emotional feelings, that was quite unfamiliar, really out of the question, something for weeds and wimps. In Steve's book, one could think of the possibility of relaxation and leisure only in retirement.

'That may be all right for some, when the time comes. For us, the most urgent thing is to get ourselves financially secure; then we may be able to begin thinking about relaxing a bit.' He appeared so deadly serious and unsmiling. His wife looked sad, resigned.

'There's no time I can afford to fool around with anything unproductive. I've got responsibility for hundreds of people under my direction. And that's quite apart from the mortgage pressures we are now under, which puts everything else on hold. I can't imagine us being able to have a holiday for quite a while yet. And I certainly don't plan to waste any precious time doing any of those foolish things my wife put on her list of leisure activities that she talked about before.'

I now knew how correct Gina's assessment of him was. Earlier, she had described Steve as 'unbending, tough, unemotional, apparently uncaring and cold'. It was clearly the time to challenge this thinking. But would he listen?

'Steve, there's lots of strong evidence that shows the benefits of shared fun experiences, especially those enjoyed with your wife and family. There are plenty of men we know at your stage of married life who have had to reassess. Many have given up the executive rat race of over-responsibility. Some have even begun to enjoy their lives again, showing the same love they used to show their wives when they first married.

'Many have learnt unselfishly to give time and respect to their wife and families — and have received back even more respect themselves! They've discovered that life is too short not to enjoy the great opportunities they've been given. Enjoying and living life like this with one's wife and family is the best reward on offer. But you'll need to be willing to change your thinking and act on it to experience the truth of what we're saying.'

As he listened and tried to speak, nothing came out at first. Finally he said, 'I'm not so sure what I think about that.' If it was true, all those walls he'd so successfully erected to prevent him from having to get too close to women, especially Gina his wife, would now be at risk.

I needed to reinforce what I had said so that he would pursue this difficult line of thinking and not look for a way out. 'Steve, all your life you've been running. Now it's time to stop. You need to face up to your humanness. Everyone is made for relationship and with that comes full emotional expression. It's part of the package. Living in relationship with Gina must start to mean much more than paying the mortgage and seeing her for breakfast.

When will you put some balance back into your lives, including some leisure, and start just having fun? It means really reassessing, asking what's right.'

Steve's struggle was intense. Although the concessions were small, it was a beginning. He agreed, with difficulty, to set aside some reasonable time on the next weekend to talk about a few of these ideas with Gina. This would include discussion of a holiday later in the year. Also on the agenda would be at least one thing they would share together that would be fun. Steve said he wouldn't guarantee this last thing, but he'd at least discuss it.

We know it is still early days for this couple. They have begun, but they will need to persevere. It will certainly require Steve to allow himself time for leisure before retirement! For Gina, the hope of having fun and some balance in her marriage has been revived.

✠ Having fun in marriage means sharing interests

Have you noticed how easy it is to lose contact with someone when your mutual interests change? Perhaps you've been seeing a friend at tennis for years and he tells you this Saturday is his last at tennis, as he's moving next week to another suburb. You sincerely say and truly mean it when you say: 'I'll really miss you, but we'll keep in touch; I'll call you in a few weeks so we can get together for coffee.'

But, somehow for a while, you both forget. And when you do eventually call, it seems good at first, but somehow the conversation soon flags. You might even meet once or twice, but ultimately the nature of such a friendship changes. Unless there is something else to keep it in place, this is inevitable.

Maintenance of a relationship requires either sharing at

least one common interest or developing a personal bond. It will also be much more lasting if that bond and interest includes fun aspects.

In the marriage relationship, it is much the same. When mismatched couples first marry, often their love will blind them from seeing the obvious. If they have few shared interests and little that they enjoy together except being physically stirred, we should not be surprised that frequently love fades. Part of the problem for many couples 'in love' is that they have a limited understanding of their mutual need to develop joint interests and to have fun together in sharing these.

When engaged couples see us to discuss their relationship and to prepare for marriage, we always ask about their shared social, cultural, leisure and sporting interests. Sometimes they have plenty in common — or, at least, a few interests they really desire to share. Then, I often find myself saying something like: 'You'll find that making an effort now to really enjoy developing shared interests will have long-term rewards. There's a wealth of fun and potential fulfilment for you as you explore what each other's interests are.'

However, at times we find couples who seem to have little fun together and don't indicate any desire to pursue joint interests. Even when we explain the importance of finding and developing at least a few things they can enjoy together, they will often remain unconvinced — that is, while their emotional state remains high. But once the early flush of love begins to fade for either one of them, it becomes easier for them to understand.

It was very like this for Alan and Nancy. She was born in outer suburban Sydney. He was born in rural England, later moving to Australia with his family when at primary school and completing his education at an agricultural school. Alan was uncertain about his natural father. 'My parents were only married a few years ago, having lived together for twenty years or so. However, my dad is not my natural father. Of the four kids, none of us has the same natural father and we are all quite different.'

Nancy, on the other hand, saw her parents as a stable and loving influence. 'Although my parents have had their share of good times and bad, I feel their commitment to stay together has given my brother and me a form of stability in our lives as we grew up.'

Coming from quite different backgrounds, but very much believing that their youthful love would be sufficient, they married young. As Nancy said: 'Our first year together was like one long honeymoon. We were both only nineteen and we thought we could enjoy our youth together.'

Well, there is nothing wrong with such a beginning, but it is then necessary to build on that and develop shared interests to help in overcoming any cultural or background differences. It seems none of these provisos eventuated for Alan and Nancy.

Nancy said: 'I had always thought our marriage could be a good one, especially in the beginning. We were both active Christians. Alan even wanted to become a pastor when we were going out. However, over the last couple of years he seems to have lost interest in his faith and I have ended up going to church by myself.

'I believe he prefers the life he lives with his workmates. Most of them are bachelors, divorced or separated from wives. His job, career and workmates are certainly first in his life and always take first priority. He seems to go to the pub most nights and is often away. At first, he let me come on his nights out; now, he never wants me to go with him.

'It's been a long time since we had any fun together.

He left me two weeks before our second baby was born.'

There was poignancy and hopelessness in the suffering she shared. We could feel Nancy's despair in her words. We ached with her as we realised the whole foundation of this marriage was wrong. It had been built not only on totally false hopes and expectations, but without any evidence of the two of them being able to enjoy shared interests.

We have observed that married couples who are balanced — fully 'earthed', yet aware spiritually — generally seem to be bright, alive folks who are capable of greatly enjoying themselves and others. Imbued with a sense of fun, they fully enjoy life and the good gifts they share and are usually fun people to be with.

Of course, they also know when to be serious. But, comfortable with their identity, able to mix freely and enjoy the company of most people in any society, they will usually have a wide variety of interests, as well as good friends to enjoy them with. These are the kind of married people whose friendship others seek and whom we would do well to emulate.

✠ Having fun and a sense of responsibility can go together

Some people seem to think that having fun and being responsible at the same time is impossible. How often do we hear: 'Now we are married, the good times have gone. It was much more fun when we were single, could live it up and stay out late.' Some seem to think of marriage as limiting, inhibiting our freedom and, especially, preventing us from having fun.

So often, perspective depends upon our early models of marriage, as well as our present maturity. Those fortunate enough to have had encouraging, supportive and well-balanced parents will know and understand how marriage and family life can combine lots of fun in balance with responsible living. Rather than feeling that marriage is restrictive and limiting upon one's enjoyment, it will be clear that marriage, because it is a shared experience, actually operates to enhance fun and enjoyment.

We know many married couples whose parents easily combine the ability to provide for them, whether as children or young adults, a secure and fun-loving home environment. Here, there is always given opportunity to welcome and enjoy their friends and visitors of all ages in an informal or social setting. Such family homes can provide a great spirit of friendliness, often associated with playing games or sporting activities as well as involvement in other shared fun experiences.

Fortunate, indeed, are those who belong in such families. In such homes, you can experience a relaxed freedom and share drinks, meals, music and other entertaining experiences. There is a prevailing sense of happy goodwill between all. Usually, there is also a feeling of order, mutual respect for others' arrangements and space, as well as good humour and an easygoing atmosphere.

Of course, we also know many homes where this is far from the pattern. And you may well want to ask why such ideal homes are not more prevalent. To this question we can only suggest a wide variety of dysfunctional factors as well as point to many inadequate models of parents.

If we consider the positive aspects of those marriages and families we've described, we find something unique. There the children, adolescents and young adults never seem to have missed out on lots of shared fun activities. At the same time, they will have experienced the security of responsible and caring parents who provided a loving yet disciplined upbringing. It seems to be the combination of these aspects which makes all the difference.

Marriage as rightly understood is designed to provide for us and our families a rich source of joy, fun and pleasure. Take time to explore all the ways you can responsibly discover what your life as a couple can provide as a source of joy for yourself and others. Again, this means being a balanced, in-focus person.

Seeing and keeping life in perspective and balance requires that we are not only motivated to keep being that sort of person, but we also keep working at exploring interesting or exciting things to share with our life-partner. It will make sense if we can regularly motivate each other. Asking, 'What have you got in mind to do to relax today?' or 'How would you like to have some fun this weekend?' can certainly help in this direction.

By now, we hope it is obvious that including fun times in our marriage is not just an optional extra. It is an essential. But it is also important that both husband and wife take responsibility for doing some of the planning. If only one partner takes the initiative or does the planning, if *he* always expects *her* to initiate or do the planning, then the task can become a chore. There is added pleasure in each doing some of the planning so that spouses can see a planned pleasant event as an act of love from their partner.

✠ A shared fun schedule for busy couples

We tend to find that busy people don't do a lot more than what they plan to do. It's nice when spontaneous, pleasurable events occur but, for the most part, it's important to plan them.

Of course, there are many ways this can be done. We suggest you get out the diary or calendar and put down for the month ahead those times when you are going to do things together. They can be high- or low-key pleasurable sharing times. Just make sure you include real fun times occasionally.

If you aren't sure what you could do, work through the following Shared Fun Activities Schedule. Husbands should circle the 'H' for any activities they would enjoy and wives 'W' for those they would enjoy. After completing the schedule this far, list all the activities you *both* circled. Put the list on your refrigerator and, with your calendar, start planning what you are going to do — and when! Oh, and don't forget. . . have fun!

Shared fun activities schedule

1.   W   H   *Going for a boat or ferry ride*
2.   W   H   *Watching TV together*
3.   W   H   *Playing tennis*
4.   W   H   *Eating out for breakfast/lunch/dinner*
5.   W   H   *Gardening or landscaping*
6.   W   H   *Reading humorous books, stories, poems to each other*
7.   W   H   *Inviting guests for dinner, or supper*
8.   W   H   *Having a picnic*
9.   W   H   *Taking photographs*
10.   W   H   *Visiting people who are shut in, or in hospital*
11.   W   H   *Praying together*
12.   W   H   *Taking a drive in the country*
13.   W   H   *Visiting the mountains*
14.   W   H   *Going fishing*
15.   W   H   *Going bowling*
16.   W   H   *Learning to do something new together*
17.   W   H   *Giving unexpected gifts*
18.   W   H   *Spending time with parents*
19.   W   H   *Solving puzzles, crosswords, or word games*
20.   W   H   *Kissing and cuddling, without sex*
21.   W   H   *Having a cappucino at a coffee shop*
22.   W   H   *Bird watching*

23.	W	H	*Playing table tennis*
24.	W	H	*Having or giving a massage*
25.	W	H	*Going dancing*
26.	W	H	*Walking barefoot at the beach or on grass*
27.	W	H	*Gathering shells, driftwood, objects of nature*
28.	W	H	*Throwing and catching a ball together*
29.	W	H	*Playing with a Frisbee*
30.	W	H	*Cleaning the house together*
31.	W	H	*Having a shower together*
32.	W	H	*Telling jokes or funny stories*
33.	W	H	*Finding a place just to sit together in the sun*
34.	W	H	*Playing golf or going to a golf-driving range*
35.	W	H	*Going to the hairdresser or beautician*
36.	W	H	*Going to a church meeting*
37.	W	H	*Giving a party*
38.	W	H	*Going camping*
39.	W	H	*Sleeping in late*
40.	W	H	*Taking a bushwalk or hike*
41.	W	H	*Going horseriding*
42.	W	H	*Having a weekend away*
43.	W	H	*Driving off the main roads — exploring new places*
44.	W	H	*Visiting the library*
45.	W	H	*Having a stimulating conversation*
46.	W	H	*Preparing new or special food*
47.	W	H	*Doing some drawing or painting*
48.	W	H	*Visiting a museum or exhibition*
49.	W	H	*Going for a ride on a motorbike*
50.	W	H	*Having a barbecue*
51.	W	H	*Visiting friends*
52.	W	H	*Selling or trading something;*

			having a garage sale
53.	W	H	Doing repairs to household items
54.	W	H	Going for a bicycle ride
55.	W	H	Writing articles, letters, reports, poems
56.	W	H	Attending an amusement park, circus, carnival
57.	W	H	Skating, roller-skating or roller-blading
58.	W	H	Going out for an ice-cream or milkshake
59.	W	H	Writing cards to someone
60.	W	H	Reading the Bible together
61.	W	H	Finding ways of encouraging people
62.	W	H	Working out a budget
63.	W	H	Talking about a hobby or special interest
64.	W	H	Spending time with close family members
65.	W	H	Having morning tea with friends
66.	W	H	Playing cards
67.	W	H	Playing board games
68.	W	H	Going to a movie
69.	W	H	Taking a nature walk
70.	W	H	Going shopping together
71.	W	H	'Striking' new plants from cuttings
72.	W	H	Making love
73.	W	H	Going somewhere to look at flowers, plants, trees
74.	W	H	Cooking a meal together
75.	W	H	Relaxing in front of a fire
76.	W	H	Rearranging the furniture
77.	W	H	Visiting garage sales, auctions
78.	W	H	Talking about old times
79.	W	H	Learning a foreign language

80.	W	H	*Looking through antique shops*
81.	W	H	*Singing in a choir or other group*
82.	W	H	*Making snacks and eating them*
83.	W	H	*Looking through photo albums together*
84.	W	H	*Playing music or listening to music*
85.	W	H	*Doing volunteer work, serving on community projects*
86.	W	H	*Listening to a good sermon*
87.	W	H	*Doing craft activities*
88.	W	H	*Surfing, scuba diving*
89.	W	H	*Entering competitions together*
90.	W	H	*Spending time at the beach*
91.	W	H	*Reading comic books or cartoon books*
92.	W	H	*Teaching someone*
93.	W	H	*Playing with pets*
94.	W	H	*Playing billiards or snooker*
95.	W	H	*Looking at the stars, identifying constellations*
96.	W	H	*Researching a topic together*
97.	W	H	*Attending a sports event*
98.	W	H	*Planning a holiday*
99.	W	H	*Being coached in something*
100.	W	H	*Taking an early morning run/walk/swim*

Questions for thought and discussion

✠ PERSONAL INVENTORY

This chapter brings to this book an important dimension which is often overlooked in marriage. Enjoying life and having fun is as important in marriage as it is for all stages of life. Of course, being married needs to be taken seriously. However, it seems that for many couples, married life has become so serious that perspective is lost. Not only are attitudes often less than positive, but having fun is also forgotten.

When did you last take time out together to really enjoy life? Is shared laughter a real part of your natural expression of the joy of living?

As you reflect on the ideas developed in this chapter, you can see whether your life is fully balanced. Consider whether it includes a good deal of fun and enjoyment. Are there clues here to the loss of some of the spark you once had in your marriage? Perhaps loss of joy, or missing out on the important element of fun is part of the answer. Better to deal with it now before some of the problems mentioned show up.

Take time now to think about ways you can improve these aspects of your life with your spouse. Remember, having fun together will involve you in sharing more interests. Individually, as well as together, reflect on and discuss the following questions:

1. What was your experience from your family of origin of sharing, or not sharing, together in fun times?

2. What messages about having fun in married life did this leave you with?

3. What activities/interests did you and your spouse enjoy together when you were courting?

4. Which of these activities and interests have you 'lost' over the years? Why?

5. What fun times do you have regularly programmed into your week?

6. On holidays, what do you and your spouse do to relax and enjoy different kinds of recreation/fun?

7. Identify two activities/interests that you would like to take up, rekindle or do more of with your spouse.

8. What blockages will you need to overcome to get one of these activities or interests going?

✠ SHARING WITH YOUR PARTNER

Your answers to these questions will help you see the extent to which your marriage includes having fun and also just how much joy you share in your marriage. As you discuss your responses with your spouse, make the effort to see just how creative you can be in developing new ideas and ways to put more enjoyment and sparkle back into your relationship.

Remember, you must plan if you are to increase your enjoyment and your fun times. Most busy people don't do a whole lot more than is planned. So, get out your diary or calendar and put down the times you're going to do things together for the month ahead that will be high-key or low-key pleasurable sharing times. If you're not sure what you could do, refer back to the 'Shared fun activities schedule' at the end of the chapter for some ideas.

✠ GROUP WORK

9. Share in the group the messages about having fun that you learned from your family of origin.

10. Discuss how important *you* see this issue of shared marital fun as being.

11. Share one fun time from your marriage. What made it special and what were the benefits of it?

12. Talk about the main problems group members have in getting a healthy balance of enjoyable times into their marriage. What can be done about these?

13. Remembering that fun times can include a wider circle of friends, consider organising an enjoyable outing or activity as a whole group.

Part D:
Storm-proofing

11

Become a team

'LOOK, THE BOTTOM LINE IS, SOMEONE'S got to be the boss.' Philip spoke strongly. He and Anthea had only been married a few months but, already, they had discovered how love can be damaged by constant arguments.

'I just want Anthea to understand,' he went on, 'that I'm not trying to be difficult. Some of the decisions I've had to make don't please me too much, either. But someone's got to make them, or we'll never get anywhere.'

It was apparent that somehow or other Philip was working from the premise that the husband was destined to be The Boss in any marriage. It seemed that he believed his wife was bound to submit to his decisions on every important issue, as well as most minor ones. There was usually little or no discussion about these issues. If Anthea had a different view or opposed Philip's ideas, he took this as rebellion on her part.

Not surprisingly, Anthea wasn't that excited about this approach to marriage. She was struggling with feelings of being unvalued, of feeling that, now that they were married, Philip somehow saw her as his chattel, someone who ought to be good and just do as she was told.

Attitudes of male dominance and superiority in marriage die hard in Western society.

'To be honest, I just feel used,' complained Stewart. 'It seems like I go to work, put in long hours, earn good money, but we never get ahead. Right now we owe more on bills than we can afford. And every time I bring the subject up, all I get is hostility. We needed the new lounge now. We needed the new curtains. There's not much affection or closeness. We don't even talk much. I feel like Kristen's just using me to buy everything she wants — and I've had enough!'

His anger, which had been quietly simmering for several years, had finally reached boiling point. From his perspective, he could see nothing but that Kristen was manipulating him, making decisions and creating consequences that he didn't like at all.

Attitudes of female control in marriage, openly observable or subtly exercised, continue with a frequency that causes concern.

Anders and Lucy were a modern couple whose relationship began like many others. As students, they shared a flat and later set up house together. Lucy explained, 'It was great, but I fell pregnant and had an abortion — something I will always regret. Only eight months later, I fell pregnant again, only this time I was determined to have my baby. We were now under pressure from our friends to get married.' Unfortunately, they didn't seem to be very well-prepared for marriage in terms of their understanding.

After nine years, Lucy came seeking counselling. By now they had two children. Certain bizarre sexual practices or 'fantasies' had been encouraged by Anders, who dominated Lucy. Although she was reluctant at first, she soon obediently fell into these ways without any objection, because she felt a bit scared of her husband and thought she ought to go along with what pleased him. The fantasies then became an essential part of their sex life.

However, in the process they lost all self-respect for each other and, finally, Lucy began a friendship which led to infidelity. Anders, in his warped way, seemed to gain perverse pleasure from hearing her talk about the affair as they made love. It was not long before Lucy lost both love and respect for her husband. Too late, Anders realised his mistake and regretted his foolish behaviour.

They had reluctantly separated, so we were exploring with Lucy some of the reasons she found it hard to trust and return to live with Anders. 'I really thought I had to go along with whatever my husband asked me to,' she said. 'But now I realise I was wrong; I feel degraded and cheap. Although I am concerned for him, I don't feel for Anders in the way I used to.' It soon became apparent that too much damage had been done to the foundations of this shaky marriage for it to ever be rebuilt. The sadness and hurt remains for all.

The examples above look to be stereotypes, but they are real. They are the sorts of aberrations that we humans try out as alternatives to developing a *team* approach in marriage. They don't work well.

The only approach that will take us towards a jointly-fulfilling, lovingly-intimate marriage is a team approach, an approach that respects and celebrates our equal status within the marriage, even though our roles and functions may vary. Approaches that build from the need for either husband or wife to be dominant and controlling end up being tissue-paper foundations. If we want to storm-proof our marriage for the years ahead, we have to be working on an equality, team-based approach.

✠ Blockages to building a marriage team
If dominance-submission models of marriage do not grow safety and closeness, why don't we more readily reject them? Why do we hang onto them? What blocks us from working to develop a model based on mutual equality?

The first blockage comes from the model of
our parents' marriage
It is important to do 'leaving' work in building a mature
marriage. We have to assess what was of value and what
was not in the pattern of our parents' marriage and we
have to make decisions about what we intend to do
differently.

If in our parents' marriage we saw an aggressive, bossy
dominance by our father or a manipulative dominance by
our mother, we have to recognise its destructiveness and
break from that pattern. That is not how it should be
done. Before blindly following their model, we need to
ask ourselves if it produced loving intimacy for them. We
need to examine the fruit before we engage in the same
approach to marital agriculture!

Breaking out of this entrapment isn't always easy. It
takes considerable, clear-sighted determination and a lot of
persistence to build differently to our parents. At times,
our attempts to adopt a more equal model may be
sabotaged by our parents themselves, either consciously or
unconsciously. But every husband, at some points, has to
make the choice *for* his spouse and *against* his parents; and
every wife has, at some points, to do the same! If the
model from our parents was one of dominance and
submission, we need to reject it.

The second blockage is our own personal batch
of insecurities
Perhaps we are afraid, at some deep level, that if we don't
assert control in the marriage, then our partner will.
Often unrecognised, this fear drives us to try to grab
power before he or she does.

When we go badly wrong, we try to justify our actions
by pointing out our partner's unsuitability for having a say

in decisions. He or she is 'dumb' or 'stupid', his or her ideas are 'ridiculous'. We attack one another, put each other down and try to establish our 'right' to be the controlling partner in the marriage enterprise. After all, we are stronger, wiser, more knowledgeable, a better judge; we never make mistakes!

Nothing could show up our insecurity more clearly than these attitudes or statements. Our constant need to criticise our spouse is like a neon sign flashing out the message: 'I don't feel so good about myself!' But, in our insecurity, don't expect us to acknowledge such a weakness. It scares us to have to be honest about our own inadequacies and fears but, the truth is, the more we take the risk, the more we create the possibility of true intimacy.

If we will not work our way past this blockage, we settle instead for a marriage devoid of the more tender emotions.

The third blockage is the fear of the work involved in building a marriage based on mutual respect and equality. We are unsure how to go about it and we fear it may be too difficult, so we settle for what we know — we try to control.

Undeniably, there is work involved. But the work is the work already described in the earlier chapters of this book. It is the work of learning to speak affirmingly, of programming in the time to do fun things together, of choosing to forgive failure and so on. It will require working out priorities to accomplish it, but there is no worthwhile alternative.

Jostling for control and seeking to be the boss simply won't take us where we want to go in marriage. Accept the work, knowing that it becomes a lot easier in the light of the benefits that come from a team approach to marriage.

All of the above — in fact, the whole enterprise of creating a mature, intimate marriage — presupposes a regular flow of honest, open communication. Only if we will take the risk and keep taking the risk of talking honestly, gently and respectfully with one another will we ever be able to work our way through issues such as our insecurities and unhelpful patterns from our parents' marriage patterns that impede intimacy and safety and so on.

When, instead of talking things through honestly, we hold lots of stuff inside — even pretending to ourselves that we do it because we don't want to worry our spouse — we simply settle for less intimacy, less team-ness. Instead, we cast our vote for more individuality, more 'control' in our hands, more 'hidden agenda' work in the marriage. And our sense of fulfilment in the marriage, consequently, suffers.

✠ Starting-points for building a marriage team

The essentials of making the marriage partnership a functional team are no different to those of team-building in any other enterprise. At work, when we join with others to form a team working on some project together, we know the essentials that enable it to work. We know the things that prevent it from reaching desired goals.

A team will not gel and achieve effectively unless we respect one another. Because every human has faults, the formation of a functional team requires that we look past the faults and identify the strengths and resources that each of us brings to the task in hand. It requires that we highlight the benefits of working together and play down the difficulties. Effective teams are made up of individuals who are able to put their own selfish desires aside in order to serve the greater needs of the team.

The marriage team requires the same emphasis. We need to make decisions to build our oneness, to be generous in overlooking each other's faults, to encourage and build each other up, to make the best use of each other's contributory strengths, to listen to one another, to cooperate in order to achieve worthwhile goals and to be prepared to sacrifice personal wants or needs at times for the good of our partner or the greater good of the marriage.

Some specific tasks in marriage, worth highlighting once more, include making a deliberate plan to grow our couple-ness as distinct from our individuality. Our individuality is not sacrificed in marriage, but it is re-balanced in order to make room for our couple-ness. There are times when we still express, and enjoy, our individuality, but we must give a high priority now to sharing, pleasing one another, simply cooperating.

This requires us to put into our diary times when we will do enjoyable things together, times when we will relax together, times and tasks which will please our partner. Out of this ground-soil, a fulfilling sense of working as a team emerges.

A concept that is helpful in building the sense of being a loving team is the concept of *quid pro quo*. This Latin phrase carries the sense of 'this for that', the sense of an equal responsibility in the marriage to do things for each other. If the flow of sacrificial contribution in the marriage is all one way, then the marriage may or may not function, but it will not function with a deep sense of intimacy, of loving closeness.

The flow needs to be a two-way one, I doing for my wife things to please and serve her, and she doing similar things for me. In such a partnership we can, at times, be ecstatic about the joy of being in love.

✠ Decision-making in the marriage team

In marriage, as in many enterprises, the best decisions will often be the result of input from both partners. When one partner operates as The Boss and tries to force decisions through with no input from his or her partner, it disrupts the sense of mutual worth in the marriage.

This is not to say, of course, that every decision has to be jointly processed. When there is a strong foundation of security and trust in the marriage, a large number of decisions can automatically be made by one partner without input from the other. The basis for being able to do this, without it being a problem, lies in the fact that the couple has reached a comfortable agreement about who has the better expertise in this particular area.

So, for example, the husband and wife may have decided that the wife handles the finances best and she will proceed to make many decisions on the basis that this is her area of responsibility. Only when there is to be a change in direction, or some new, significant decision is to be made, do they need to consult and talk the issue through. Mature marriages have a fairly clear definition of who is responsible for what. They proceed well because the two marriage partners carry out their responsibilities reliably.

But with new or important decisions, the decision-making process involves listening to each other respectfully. When there are different points of view and disagreement about the best plan of action, the couple are able to handle the situation without either feeling walked all over. The process is one in which each has input, each feels listened to and, even when a decision is made that is not the preferred choice for both partners, there is a sense in which that is okay because there is a rough equality across the broad range of decisions; neither feels unfairly treated. He gets his preference sometimes; she gets hers at other times; and that enables the marriage to work with a sense of mutual fulfilment.

Where decisions are particularly big or emotive, the best plan is to take time, as much as this is possible. It is useful to list the options on paper, giving each person the opportunity to put the case for their particular viewpoint and leaving time to weigh things up. If the process is handled with respect for my ideas and I feel listened to, then even if the final decision is not the one I would prefer, I will usually be able to live with it more comfortably. I can recognise that sometimes my marriage can only move ahead by one of us putting aside our wishes on a particular issue. If we both 'win' from time to time, then resentment rarely becomes a problem. On the other hand, if the same person always gets his or her way, there is a significant likelihood of resentment building.

Attempting decision-making, following this approach, will mean we reduce conflicts and emotionally-debilitating arguments to a minimum. Most of the important decisions we make will reflect the input of both of us.

✠ Different roles in the marriage team

Is it possible to carry out different roles, yet still have a sense of functioning as a loving team, in the marriage? Of course it is. Just as effective teams in any arena of life are made up of individuals carrying out different roles, yet working together for the overall goal, so this same model works well in marriage.

Perhaps a few roles are pre-set. The wife alone can bear children. And, normally, the earliest nurturing of the children will be done by the wife. However, beyond this, there can be considerable flexibility. We would certainly see it as important that the husband also be actively involved in the nurturing role with children, at times perhaps being the primary caregiver.

Having a child is an exciting, significant undertaking! There is no way that it should be less than a team enterprise, both in terms of the work involved in nurturing and instructing and in terms of the joys involved in seeing milestones passed in the child's life.

Other roles need to be talked through, so that joint decisions are made. Who is better suited to handle the weekly shopping, the gardening, the maintenance of the car, the heavy cleaning work, the budgeting, making curtains, cooking, playing the role of 'the kitchen fairy' and so on? Perhaps some of these roles can be shared. Perhaps some of them can become fun times, joint enterprises — cleaning · the house together on Saturday mornings or doing some late-night shopping together (followed by a cappucino)!

Once again, the key task is to talk openly and honestly together so that each has the opportunity to contribute on his or her likes, dislikes, areas of competence and areas of incompetence — and to feel listened to.

Some roles in the running of the household are simply not destined to be fun. Very few people enjoy cleaning the toilet and bathroom. Yet someone has to do these tasks. The dividing up of tasks and the taking on of roles, even some unpleasant ones, becomes no big deal when we feel supported and appreciated, with a sense of fairness operating in the team.

Most times, the workable solution will involve a combination of approaches, in which each partner takes on some roles that they have some competence in and/or enjoy. Each takes on some less pleasant roles and some roles are shared. Occasional reassigning of roles can be helpful.

The vital components, once again, include keeping the communication lines open and appreciating and supporting each other's contributions, rather than focussing on imperfections. This basic approach enables the married couple to function as an effective and successful team.

✠ Dominance reversal in the marriage team

In this chapter, there has been a significant emphasis on the importance of fairness in the assigning of tasks and roles and the importance of recognising each other's equality in the marriage, as opposed to seeing one as The Boss.

This emphasis is deliberate. These are very important guidelines. Yet they can be misconstrued. The marriage can be viewed as some kind of business deal to which each contributes fifty per cent. Partners can end up keeping either a mental or an actual tally sheet, showing how they are doing more than their partner. They can use this approach to pressure their partner into doing more for them.

Wrong! A marriage that is, ultimately, no more than a business deal can never be much more than a miserable marriage.

The best marriage will go considerably beyond this foundation of equality and become a kind of competition in dominance reversal! In this marriage, both partners will make considerable efforts to sacrifice their own needs out of love for their spouse. They will seek to take on more than their fair share of the work in running the household. They will gladly undertake roles that they don't particularly like doing in order to save their partner from having to do them.

This improved model runs, really, on a foundation of self-sacrifice. The centre of the marriage is marked by a kind of fun competition in which each partner seeks, in love, to *outgive* their spouse. Wherever this approach operates, everybody wins.

Humans continue to seek for alternatives to loving, sharing, cooperating, affirming. In marriage, as in most other areas of life, the alternatives exist, but they don't build fulfilling, intimate marriages!

Sadly, male chauvinism is alive and well in much of our society still. The feminist movement found its impetus in the attitude of men who too often thought they had some kind of divine mandate to live out male superiority. They never did and still don't — and their position still remains, at base, an expression of self! If these words appear strong, it is because they reflect some of the misuse of women in marriage that we see in our clinics as individuals and couples come, seeking help.

But it is equally true that we see many marriages where the wife has played the role of The Boss, sometimes overtly, often more subtly. It doesn't matter how the role is played — it doesn't work. Pairing dominance and passivity can produce a workable marriage, but it will never produce one where each feels safe and valued and, hence, is able to share at the deepest levels of intimacy.

So, our message is really a call! It is a call to men and women to take a long, hard look, not at how their spouse is functioning in the marriage, but at how they are doing. It is a call to renew their determination to build an equality — or, better, a favouring of the other — in the marriage. It is a call to work towards becoming a loving team, putting in the groundwork necessary for this model.

A marriage that is a loving team can, in the end, handle the storms of life better than any other alternative.

Questions for thought and discussion

✠ PERSONAL INVENTORY

In this chapter, your marriage has been given a new perspective. There is a call to both of you to become 'team players'.

In too many marriages, there can be inequality coupled with little respect. In these situations, without warning, a storm can blow up and hurts can easily be generated. These can arise from a deep sense of unfairness associated with inequality.

Do you have some rethinking to do to correct your concepts and ideas of the truth? If so, please take time out now to apply the principles from this chapter. In the end, you might even have to change what you believed and justified as the model for your marriage. As you make the effort now to replace wrong thinking and foolish actions, you will be storm-proofing your marriage and providing lasting protection for the future.

1. What model for a husband and wife relating together did you see in your parents' marriage?

2. To what extent do you think you have, uncritically, taken the same model into your marriage?

3. How has the model 'inherited' from your parents worked in terms of your and your spouse's fulfilment?

4. What model of marriage has the media promoted over the years? To what extent has this affected you?

5. Think about some of the people who acted as role models in your teenage years (and beyond) on which you have developed your ideas of equality in marriage. How helpful, unhelpful or influential has this been?

6. To what extent do you support and encourage your spouse in your marriage?

7. To what extent do you *feel* supported and encouraged by your spouse?

8. Why does domination or attempts to exert control over the other partner cause damage? How can this be corrected?

9. When both husband and wife are working outside the home, what are your views about who does the household chores?

10. In your marriage, whose occupation is considered to be the more important? Why?

11. How do you go about making important decisions? Do you always manage to have joint agreement? If not, what happens?

✠ SHARING WITH YOUR PARTNER

Take time to share with each other your answers to the questions above. Make sure you put the emphasis on listening and understanding each other, not changing each other.

Ask yourselves: 'What can we do to develop more of a team model within our marriage?' And plan together to take action on ideas that you generate.

✠ GROUP WORK

12. How relevant today is the traditional view that 'a woman's place is in the home'?

13. A sharp tongue, anger, manipulation, withdrawal, nagging — these and many other methods are used by people to control the marriage. Unfortunately, all of them destroy intimacy and trust. Why are we so afraid to aim for joint control and equality in the marriage partnership?

14. What actions have been helpful in your marriage in developing a sense of equal importance? Discuss.

15. What blockages to joint decision-making in your marriage have you encountered? Discuss ways of handling these better.

16. Share on a hard but good decision that you jointly made. What enabled you to handle this decision well?